Meeting the Standards

Improving Middle Level Teacher Education

National Middle School Association is dedicated to improving the educational experiences of young adolescents by providing vision, knowledge, and resources to all who serve them in order to develop healthy, productive, and ethical citizens.

Library of Congress Cataloging-in-Publication Data

Swaim, John.

   Meeting the standards : improving middle level teacher education / John H. Swaim, Greg P. Stefanich.

       p.   cm.

   Includes bibliographical references (p.)

   1. Middle school teachers–Training of–United States.

I. Stefanich, Greg. II. National Middle School Association.

III. Title.

LB1735.5.S83   1996

370.71–dc20

Meeting the Standards:

Improving Middle Level Teacher Education

John H. Swaim
Greg P. Stefanich

National Middle School Association
Columbus, Ohio

NMSA

John Swaim and Greg Stefanich are members of NMSA's Professional Preparation and Certification Committee which sponsored this study. Dr. Swaim is Professor of Education Emeritus, University of Northern Colorado, and Dr. Stefanich is Professor of Education, University of Northern Iowa, Cedar Falls.

This important study is another indication of National Middle School Association's commitment to work toward the achievement of more appropriate teacher education for middle level educators. The association is grateful to Drs. Swaim and Stefanich for conceiving of and conducting this project, the first of its kind. The results will provide needed guidance to the increasing number of institutions of higher education that are developing distinctive preparation programs for middle level educators.

Copyright© 1996
National Middle School Association
2600 Corporate Exchange Drive, Suite 370
Columbus, Ohio 43231

ISBN 1-56090-107-1
Printed in the United States of America

Contents

Foreword

In 1990 the National Council for Accreditation of Teacher Education (NCATE) established, for the first time, national standards for the accreditation of programs designed to prepare teachers for the middle grades. The National Middle School Association (NMSA) as a constituent member of NCATE was responsible for researching, preparing, and forwarding for approval the guidelines that NCATE put into effect in 1990. NMSA's Professional Preparation and Certification Committee provided the leadership in the development of these new guidelines.

The Professional Preparation and Certification Committee is pleased to sponsor this publication, *Meeting the Standards: Improving Middle Level Teacher Education,* to assist those who are establishing or redesigning programs aimed at providing better prepared middle grades teachers. This monograph adds a new dimension to the increasing flow of work on middle level teacher education that has characterized the decade of the 90s. In the text and reference list of this documents you will encounter the names of Ken McEwin, Tom Dickinson, and Peter Scales, each of whom has made multiple contributions to the expanding knowledge base on teacher education. In addition, the May 1995 issue of the *Middle School Journal* addressed the need for better middle grades teacher education with a nine article focus section entitled "Reforming Middle Grades Teacher Preparation."

Complementing what has gone before, this work by John Swaim and Greg Stefanich makes a unique contribution to the literature. Swaim and Stefanich have chosen to organize their monograph around the NCATE standards. For every standard required for approval of a middle level teacher education program, they have provided concrete examples of how various programs have chosen to meet that standard. In that process thirty-nine different teacher education programs are sampled. These programs have been developed in a variety of settings: regional institutions, comprehensive universities, liberal arts colleges, and research institutions.

Teacher education exists in a dynamic world, so it is not surprising that In 1995 the standards for middle level teacher education, although approved initially only five years ago, have undergone a revision. Through an important epilogue and appendices that include the new revised standards together with charts that indicate how each standard has been effected in the revision, Swaim and Stefanich have kept this monograph current with this changing world of accreditation standards. Consequently, *Meeting the Standards* will provide guidance for those seeking to create or revise middle grades teacher education programs for years to come.

Thomas O. Erb
Editor, *Middle School Journal*
and Former Chairman,
Professional Preparation and
Certification Committee

Prologue

As the professional association whose prime purpose is the promotion of developmentally appropriate education for young adolescents, National Middle School Association has been a long-standing advocate of preparing, licensing, and certifying middle level educators. This monograph is yet another example of NMSA's commitment to and leadership in the special preparation of middle level teachers.

Educators have recognized for decades that students in the middle grades are unique in their developmental characteristics and learning needs (Douglas, 1920; Van Til, Lounsbury, Vars, 1961; Eichhorn, 1966; Alexander, 1968). Yet, despite this awareness, very little has been done by universities or state boards of education to ensure that middle schools are staffed with personnel who are prepared to work with this challenging age group (Scales & McEwin, 1994; McEwin & Dickinson, 1995).

Lack of middle level licensure and certification, transfer of teachers to different buildings within a school district, and hiring preferences by school officials often result in many middle level schools being staffed with teachers who have neither knowledge of young adolescents nor understanding of curriculum organization and instructional strategies that are appropriate for this age group. There are far too many middle level educators who still have little understanding of the developmental nature of young adolescents. They may know how young adolescents behave, but often do not understand why the choices students make are not consistent with adult expectations. Likewise, such educators are making curricular and instructional decisions without a knowledge base or the preparation needed to do so. On the other hand, there are a growing number of those who do recognize the importance of early adolescence and are taking advantage of middle level teacher preparation programs and other professional development opportunities now beginning to emerge in middle level education.

The staffing of middle level classrooms with teachers interested in and prepared to teach other levels continues to be a problem. Historically, teacher preparation institutions, state departments of education, and the profession itself have failed to provide specially designed programs to prepare teachers and other professionals for careers in middle level education. Since the founding of the junior high school movement at the beginning of this century, middle level schools have been staffed by persons whose preparation and interest lie at other levels.

Aubrey Douglas, an early advocate of the junior high, recognized as early as 1920 that one of the major causes that would lead to the failure of the junior high would be that: "teachers are inadequately trained for the junior high school (most received their formal education in subject matter rather than knowledge of student development; few discharged their role of guiding teenagers)" (Douglas, 1920).

Unfortunately, the same type of criticism Douglas made regarding the preparation of junior high teachers in 1920 can be made about the preparation of middle level teachers today, a situation that could also well lead to the failure of the middle school, as it did the junior high.

In an effort to avoid the fate of the junior high, middle level education today must address and resolve the issue of preparing teachers whose primary focus is the education of young adolescents. This monograph will assist colleges and universities in their efforts to meet this responsibility. Failure to do so may result in the middle school being a valid educational ideal but without the personnel to carry it out.

Meeting the Standards will not only help colleges and universities establish middle level teacher education programs, but it will also help those with already established programs improve their programs.

McEwin (1992) identified 243 higher education institutions who claimed that they had some type of middle school teacher education program. These and other schools were invited to describe how their programs met specific NMSA/NCATE middle level teacher education guidelines. There were 78 schools that submitted examples of their middle school teacher education programs. Of those 78, the vast majority submitted examples for only their undergraduate programs. However, there were a few schools that submitted examples covering both their basic and advanced programs. Of the schools that submitted their advanced program examples, almost all were at the master's level. From the 78 responses, 39 schools ultimately were selected for citation in this report.

Just as there are different ways of creating an effective middle school, so too there are different ways to create a middle school teacher education program. All of the programs cited in this monograph have one common purpose: preparing teachers to work with young adolescents in a developmentally appropriate educational environment. Although this common bond exists among the schools, each school approaches meeting the various NMSA/NCATE guidelines in different ways. Thus, we were able to give at least two examples for each guideline at the basic and masters levels. In addition to the Basic and Masters Guidelines, programs which addressed, or are beginning to address, the Specialist and Doctoral Guidelines are also cited. However, because of the lack of such programs, specific descriptions of how institutions address each of the NMSA/NCATE Specialist and Doctoral Guidelines are not described. Instead, an overall summary of each of these levels is given, citing institutions who have developed or are currently developing programs.

In addition to the four levels addressed in the NMSA/NCATE guidelines, one other area of preparation emerged during this study. Although this area has no official guidelines, it serves a distinct purpose for a number of institutions. At some institutions it is called a Fifth Year Program, and it leads to initial licensure. At other institutions it is called a MAT Program that not only leads to initial licensure, but also to a masters degree. Still other institutions refer to it as a Post Baccalaureate Program which may include graduate or undergraduate credit for licensure, with the graduate credit often counting toward an advanced degree. Because there are no specific guidelines for this diverse area, it will be summarized in a similar way to the specialist and doctoral levels.

The project that resulted in this publication was guided by the following strongly held beliefs:

1. Middle level education will not reach its full potential if higher education and state departments of education fail to recognize the importance of preparing teachers specifically for the middle level.

2. The NMSA/NCATE middle school teacher education guidelines provide valid standards by which programs preparing middle school teachers can be assessed.

3. There are sufficient numbers of middle level teacher education programs now in existence that can provide guidance and direction for other colleges and universities that wish to develop effective programs of their own.

4. There are a growing number of teacher educators who also believe in the importance of preparing middle level teachers and who would like to enhance their program or would like to start a program at their own institution.

From these four underlying beliefs the following purposes were established for this monograph:

1. To recognize higher education institutions which are currently taking a lead in the preparation of middle level teachers.

2. To encourage other institutions to establish middle level teacher education programs.

3. To give examples of how middle school teacher education programs can meet the NMSA/NCATE Guidelines.

4. To provide a network among middle level teacher education programs that would promote the preparation of middle level teachers.

Although much in this monograph is encouraging, a monumental task still confronts those involved in teacher education if we are going to make the needed impact on the preparation of middle level teachers. This report is not only written to give the readers a sense of satisfaction that we are moving in the right direction, but also to challenge them to act on behalf of middle school teacher education and, ultimately, middle level education itself. ■

1. *Professional Preparation and Middle Level Education*

Teacher Education

If the preparation of middle level teachers is not addressed, we surely run the risk of losing the tremendous gains made during the last three decades in establishing an educational environment designed to meet the developmental needs of young adolescents. If Aubrey Douglas were to investigate the status of middle level education today, he would still find that middle level teachers are not being adequately prepared, although he would find some satisfaction knowing that progress has been made toward resolving this situation. Several significant events have occurred in the last few years which would indicate real strides are being made in the preparation of teachers for the middle level.

- A majority of the states now have some type of middle level licensure/certification.

- There are now NCATE guidelines for middle level undergraduate, masters, specialist and doctoral programs (NMSA, 1991).

- Several significant studies have been done on middle level teacher education and certification (see second section of Chapter 2).

- NMSA issued a position paper supporting the preparation and certification of middle level educators (NMSA, 1991).

- The National Association of State Directors of Teacher Education and Certification adopted middle level outcome-based standards to assist states in developing consistent middle level certification standards (NASDTEC, 1993).

- The National Board for Professional Teaching Standards has formed several committees to develop standards specifically to address various areas of middle level teaching (NBPTS, 1992).

Although these are all encouraging signs that middle level teacher education is at last being addressed, the problem is far from being resolved.

There are still many obstacles to overcome before we can say that our young adolescents are being taught by well-prepared and committed teachers. In fact, as so aptly suggested by the title of Peter Scales' (1992) recent study, these events merely offer *Windows of Opportunity to Improve Middle Grades Teacher Preparation.* By not taking advantage of these windows of opportunity, the education opportunities and welfare of millions of young adolescents are hanging in the balance. We must take advantage of these windows of opportunity. These youth need and deserve developmentally responsible schools staffed with knowledgeable and capable teachers who are experts at their profession, not strangers to middle level classrooms and the young adolescents who spend much of their lives there (McEwin & Dickinson, 1995).

A survey by the National Association of Secondary School Principals in 1981 showed that 41% of the principals stated that their teachers had no specific training for the middle level. This is not surprising. Scales and McEwin (1994) reported in a study that only a small percentage of the 2139 middle school teachers they surveyed reported that there were any types of middle level preparation programs available to them during their initial preparation.

This becomes more significant (or insignificant, depending on how one views it) when one realizes that the small percentage of those teachers that did have some type of formal preparation most likely received their preparation from universities that were themselves inadequately qualified to address the full scope of the NMSA/NCATE guidelines. The results of Scales' (1992) study document show a slight increase in the number of middle level teacher education programs in the last few years but also suggest that the quality of many of these programs is still questionable. This fact is affirmed when one looks at the number of middle level teacher education programs that have actually received approval after submitting their program for the NMSA/NCATE folio review approval. One third of the middle level teacher education programs that submitted folios for review did not meet the NMSA/NCATE guidelines (Swaim,1993).

TABLE 1

Percent of Middle Level Schools by Different Grade Organizations and Total Sample Having Faculties with Various Extents of Special Middle Level Preparation (1988)

Percents	Percent of Schools in 1988 Survey				Total Sample
	Grades 5-8	Grades 6-8	Grades 7-8	Grades 7-9	
Less than 25%	66	61	57	46	56
25% to 50%	14	16	16	17	17
50% to 75%	9	15	13	11	13
75% to 100%	11	8	15	25	13

(Alexander & McEwin, 1989, p. 42).

Table 1 supports the notion that many teachers currently staffing middle schools have had little formal preparation regarding programs and practices that are associated with good middle level education. In addition to these new programs and practices, there has also been a move to shift the curriculum at the middle level from subject-centered to a more integrated and skill-centered program (Lounsbury, 1992; Stevenson, 1992; Beane, 1993; Brazee/Capelluti, 1995). The widely cited *Turning Points : Preparing American Youth for the Twenty-first Century* (Carnegie, 1989) also calls for middle schools to involve parents and the community. Although many middle level teachers may be aware of these educational practices, a commitment to put them into action in the classroom is often lacking.

A middle level school organizational structure has become the predominant form of school organization through which students ages 10-14 enter high school (Epstein & Mac Iver, 1990). Unfortunately, teacher preparation programs have not kept pace with the growing number of teachers needed for middle level schools. The estimated 12,000 middle level schools continue to be staffed, mostly with teachers and other personnel prepared for teaching at other levels (Scales & McEwin, 1994).

Are there programs available to prepare educators who wish to work in a middle level setting? Early studies by Alexander and McEwin (1982, 1988) were anything but reassuring as only 30% of higher education institutions offered special preparation programs for the middle level in 1986-87, based on 715 American Association for the Accreditation of Teacher Educators member institutions surveyed. From data gathered five years earlier, almost the same percentage of these same institutions provided any special type of preparation program for middle level educators. According to a survey done in 1992, 34% of higher education institutions now had middle level teacher education programs, a slightly encouraging figure (McEwin, 1992). This minimal growth, however, indicates that colleges and universities still give priority to preparing elementary and secondary teachers, while those who desire work in the middle grades continue to be shortchanged.

Some institutions surveyed expressed disappointment at the low student enrollment when such programs were available, which indicated that if states do not provide special certification for middle level educators, there is very little incentive for students to take specific middle level course work. Scales (1992), in citing research conducted by Little and Shulman, identifies the following factors as being important to begin or sustain a middle grades program:

—whether states require separate and unique middle-grades certification;

— whether schools and districts see a need for more middle-grades teachers;

— the current priorities of the higher education institution;

— whether there are adequate numbers of students who enroll in the middle-grades program; and

— whether middle-grades issues are congruent with the research and teaching interests of individual faculty members (Scales,1992, p.46).

TABLE 2
Number and Percent of Institutions Having
Special Preparation Programs for the Middle Level

	1981-82	1986-87	1990-91
Number of Respondents	538	504	715
Number Having Programs	162	168	243
Percent Having Programs	30%	33%	34%

(McEwin & Alexander, 1982, 1988; McEwin, 1992.)

Both middle school teachers and principals tend to favor additional course work as the avenue through which special certification should be obtained rather than receiving a separate degree. They strongly favor course work in areas of young adolescent development, curriculum management, and field experiences with middle level students. These preferred courses and experiences are similar to those suggested by contemporary middle grades experts who also advocate special certification for middle grade personnel (McEwin & Allen, 1983).

The fact that both middle school teachers and principals favor taking additional course work to attain the knowledge base needed for working with young adolescents in place of a special degree is somewhat in contrast to claims made previously by middle level experts, who emphasized the need for special degree programs (DeMedio & Stewart, 1990).

Teacher preparation institutions have been reluctant to establish middle level programs without matching certification. Likewise, certification agencies have permitted teachers with a great variety of preparations to teach in the middle grades without penalty. This situation has created, or at least perpetuated, one of the most serious problems in middle level education – that of making middle level schools miniature versions of senior high schools or upward extensions of elementary schools. Middle level schools are often perceived by some as just a holding pen in between the elementary and high schools. Recently, however, more and more middle level schools are being transformed into distinct educational entities with identities of their own, thus becoming a key link in the K-12 educational system. Irvin (1992) suggests that middle schools must engage in "the deeper process of transformation – altering the fundamental character or identity." If middle level schools are to experience such a transformation, it only stands to reason that they must be staffed with teachers who understand and appreciate the importance of middle level education.

The problem created by a lack of specialized middle level teacher preparation programs at the undergraduate level has been compounded by the fact that colleges and universities have not met the challenge of establishing such programs at the graduate level. Those who choose a middle level teaching career often find it difficult, indeed at times impossible, to find graduate programs which focus on teaching young adolescents. A 1992 survey by McEwin of 243 schools which had some type of middle level teacher preparation program identified only 7% that had specialization at the masters level in middle level education and 6% that had specialization beyond a masters. These numbers fall far short of meeting the needs of middle level teachers who are seeking masters degrees in middle level education or seeking graduate level courses to renew their certification (McEwin, 1992).

Specialized middle level preparation is also needed beyond the masters and specialists levels. As middle level education continues to grow in stature and prominence in American education, the need for educational leaders in areas such as curriculum development, staff development, and teacher preparation becomes even more crucial. Doctoral programs will ensure that teachers who are striving toward leadership positions in middle level education will have rich opportunities to enhance their knowledge of the field. Doctoral programs will also be self-fulfilling with respect to middle level teacher education, because they will produce a new (possibly the first) generation of middle level teacher educators especially prepared in middle level education pedagogy.

While the literature supports the uniqueness of middle level students in physical, intellectual, and social/emotional areas (Beane & Lipka, 1987; Van Hoose & Strahan, 1988; Scales, 1991), little has been done to ensure that educators are adequately prepared to best accommodate these needs in the classroom. With the increased demand for accountability and the complex developmental and learning needs of students in middle level schools, it is crucial that those who work with young adolescents be professionally prepared. Educators need the necessary breadth and depth of understanding of this age and the curricular and instructional implications of that knowledge to ensure successful learning experiences for 10-15 year olds (NMSA, 1991, 1995).

The need for caring adult role models is more critical today for young adolescents than ever before. During the 1980s, single parent homes have increased more than 90%, and one out of every three of those homes exists at or below the poverty level. Today most youngsters have less contact with adults outside of the school environment than at any previous time in history. This change places tremendous responsibility on middle level educators, who may be the only adults available to nurture social and emotional development on a consistent basis (Toepfer, 1986, NMSA, 1995).

In turn, this places responsibility on higher education to prepare teachers who are committed and prepared to work with this critical age level. We must face this challenge now rather than later, not only because young adolescents are at risk, but because a supportive climate for reform in teacher education is imminent. Now is the time to take advantage of this reform movement called for by such prominent educators as John Goodlad (1990) in his book *Teachers For Our Nation's Schools*. Middle level educators have a golden opportunity to capitalize on this general reform movement as a means of establishing distinctive middle level teacher education programs.

Endorsement, Licensure, Certification, and Accreditation

Two essential elements in any profession are the process by which one enters a field and the means the profession uses to maintain high standards. The teaching profession is no exception. Examples of this in other professions include: having an area of endorsement that gives you special qualifications to do a particular job, having met certain criteria that allows you to practice a certain profession, having achieved certain standards that allow you to advance professionally, or having your place of employment recognized as a place where quality work is done.

In the field of education, as opposed to most professions, these processes are generally controlled by state government agencies rather than at a national level by the profession itself. Although this assures more local control, it often creates inconsistency with regard to implementation and enforcement. The issue of state versus national control of education is not as critical as are the issues of consistency in the process of endorsing, licensing, and certifying teachers as well as accrediting teacher education programs.

The processes of endorsing, licensing, certifying, and accrediting are critical elements when discussing teacher education. Each of these areas must be examined with respect to middle level teacher education if one is to fully understand the importance of the preparation of teachers for the middle level. The following section will distinguish between these four processes, realizing by doing so the distinction that is made may be inconsistent with how some states might define these same processes. However, an attempt has been made to define these processes in terms of current national trends and research in the area of teacher education.

- **Endorsement:** An area of expertise added to a primary area of teaching (middle school endorsement added to elementary license, mathematics endorsement added to science certificate, etc.)

- **License:** Initial credential needed to teach

- **Certification:** Meeting standards that qualify for professional advancement in the field of teaching

- **Accreditation:** Meeting professional standards that assure a quality education for the students within a collegiate program

Licensure

A major issue nationally is appropriate licensing for middle school teachers, counselors, and administrators. Although there is some progress in teacher licensure, standards for middle level administrators and counselors are generally nonexistent. A compounding problem is that there appears to be significant resistance toward separate middle level licensure among educators who are currently teaching, administering, or counseling in middle level schools who have never been licensed or do not possess middle level certification themselves. Also organizations that represent specific subject areas, some of which provide K-12 licensure, have been reticent in support of separate licensing for middle level educators (DeMedio & Stewart, 1990).

Although all states currently have significant numbers of middle schools, only 16 states and the District of Columbia offer middle level licensure. Of the remaining 34 states, 16 offer a middle level endorsement while 18 do not offer any middle level licensure or endorsement (Burnkrant, 1991). In those states without middle level licensure, teacher preparation institutions are not necessarily prompted to initiate programs for middle level teachers. A survey completed by McEwin (1992) found that 82%

of all middle school teacher preparation programs were found in states where middle level licensing/endorsement was available. This study further found that 57% of all middle level teacher education programs were found in the five states that required middle level licensing in order to teach at the middle level (McEwin, 1992).

In 1968, only two states offered middle level licensure (Pumerantz, 1969). By 1978, 15 states had endorsed specialized professional preparation (Gillan, 1982). In 1990, 28 states required middle level licensure/endorsement with an additional nine states reporting that licensure/endorsement was under study (McEwin, 1992). A more recent study on middle level licensing/ endorsement shows a slight increase with a total of 33 states which have now adopted some form of middle level licensing/endorsement (Valentine & Morgar, 1992). Thus, even though national momentum has been slow, more than $^2/_3$ of the states now have standards for those who teach in middle level schools. However, most of these standards are still optional and overlap secondary and elementary standards. The task that remains is to provide states not now offering middle level licensure with necessary information and research data so they will institute middle level licensure while at the same time encourage those states that have some form of middle level licensure to strengthen their standards.

A national survey, conducted by DeMedio and Stewart (1990), to determine the attitudes of middle school teachers and principals toward middle grade certification/licensure, revealed results both interesting and contradictory. A questionnaire was mailed to 2876 randomly selected elementary, middle, and secondary schools that included grades six, seven, and eight in 30 randomly selected states. A total of 1513 usable questionnaires were returned, representing a 53% response rate. The questionnaire contained 20 items with a five-point Likert scale. Fifteen items were designed to measure opinions regarding which areas should be covered during certification/licensure preparation; three items were designed to measure opinions regarding which school personnel should receive the middle grades certification/licensure; and two were designed to ascertain how respondents thought certification/licensure should be granted.

The teachers and principals presently working in middle schools across the country held similar beliefs about middle grades certification/licensure issues. Both groups believed that special certification/licensure for counselors and teachers would result in a more positive learning experience for young adolescents. Teachers also favored certification/licensure for principals, while as a group, principals did not perceive that special certification/licensure would enhance their positions as educational leaders.

Research surveys such as those cited have provided substantial data that document the growth in state certification requirements since the 1960s. While there is still much work to be done before all states provide middle level educators with the professional preparation they need, advocates have made progress in influencing attitudes through articles, conferences, publications, and public relations activities.

While the literature supports the appropriateness of middle level licensure to accommodate the unique learning needs of young adolescents, it is evident that there are obstacles to overcome before this goal will be attained. The first step toward this accomplishment must be to gain support from policy makers and those who have the power to implement changes at the state level.

State departments of education must be lobbied so that support will be forthcoming for staffing middle level schools with qualified educators, rather than with those who are there out of necessity or because of staff reassignments within the district. The efforts to lobby state legislatures for middle level licensing can best be accomplished through collaboration among higher education institutions, state middle school and professional associations, and school districts. In addition to research that supports a stand for middle level licensing, there are also influential publications that will support special preparation for middle level teachers. Some of the more notable documents published in the last few years that strongly support the special preparation of middle level teachers are listed with brief descriptions below.

- *National Middle School Association/National Council for the Accreditation of Teacher Education - Approved Curriculum Guidelines.* These guidelines have not only been used to help establish middle level teacher education programs on campuses throughout the nation, but have been used to help states develop middle school licensing standards for their state. They also provide the template around which this monograph is written.

- *National Association of State Directors of Teacher Education and Certification Outcomes-Based Standards and Portfolio Assessment.* NASDTEC represents the state certification departments across the nation. Their guidelines were rewritten in 1993 to reflect more outcomes-based standards. In that document an entire section was devoted to outcomes that address licensing guidelines for middle level teacher education.

- *Turning Points: Preparing American Youth for the Twenty-first Century.* This report, released in 1989 by the Carnegie Corporation, has been one of the major influences on the middle school movement. The Carnegie Council's Task Force on Adolescent Development made eight recommendations regarding the improvement of education for young adolescents. One of those recommendations stated that "teachers in the middle grades should be selected and specially prepared to teach young adolescents" (p. 59).

- *Interstate New Teacher Assessment and Support Consortium.* Growing concern for consistency (not necessarily national conformity nor national control) in the initial preparation and licensing of teachers has led the Council for Chief State School Officers to sponsor the study and development of outcomes for initial licensing of teachers. Although this study is still in its early stages, one of the groups under consideration for special licensing is teachers of young adolescents.

In light of research and recommendations made in the documents listed above; middle level licensure should not be negotiable, it should be a certainty. By leaving to chance the possibility that young adolescents who need special understanding the most may receive it the least, educators risk losing the potential contributions of students who may be forever lost in a world they perceive as uncaring, unaccommodating, or unchallenging.

Certification

In the previous section, certification and licensing were often referred to in the same context. This is due to the fact that they are often used by states in the same context to describe the same process of credentialing teachers. However, certification and licensing are beginning to take on a separate identity in many states. One of the major influences that has caused states to reconsider these two processes as separate entities is the work done by the National Board for Professional Teaching Standards. The board is currently developing national certification standards for teachers already in the field. The National Board has drawn a distinction between licensing teachers who are entering the teaching field and certifying teachers already in the field who are striving to meet more rigorous professional standards. Thus, certification is taking on a much different connotation as a means for experienced teachers to advance in the teaching profession rather than as solely addressing beginning teachers seeking to enter the profession.

In developing the standards and procedures for national certification, the National Board was confronted early on with the issue of what levels should be considered. An innovative approach was taken to address this issue, one which middle level educators have advocated for many years. Instead of dividing the levels for which teachers would be considered for certification by grade levels, they divided the levels by developmental stages of growth and development. Once again, the need for teachers of young adolescents was affirmed.

Further affirmation of the importance of middle level certified teachers became even more apparent when the National Board selected the Middle Level Generalist and the Middle Level Language Arts Standards as the first standards to be developed. Because these were the first to be developed, states now have the opportunity to re-examine middle level licensing and/or certification utilizing NBPT Standards as examples for developing their own middle level standards.

Accreditation

Although accreditation does not directly deal with the licensing or certification of teachers, it does impact significantly the programs teachers come from and work in. There are a variety of accrediting agencies whose prime purpose is to establish standards by which the quality of the programs within their profession can be judged. There are two types of accrediting processes which set standards directly affecting the quality of middle level education.

First, there are state and regional accrediting processes to which middle schools themselves are accountable. Many, if not most, of the state accrediting standards, however, do not directly address middle school education as a separate identity within the K-12 system. There are also regional accrediting agencies such as the North Central Association of Schools and Colleges that have developed middle level standards, but participation by schools is voluntary; and in an era of tight school finances, such external evaluation may be bypassed.

A second accrediting process deals with the preparation of middle level teachers. Although some states have developed middle level teacher preparation guidelines for accrediting middle level teacher preparation programs, the NMSA/NCATE guidelines have provided by far the most widely used process for accrediting middle level programs. It is hoped and expected that by applying these guidelines to teacher education programs throughout the nation our middle schools will eventually have a significant pool of teachers who are dedicated and committed to the education of young adolescents.

Working Together to Improve Middle Level Education

One concept that is constantly stressed in middle level education is the idea of collaboration. The literature is replete with examples of collaboration between teachers and students, students and students, teachers and teachers, teachers and administration, school and parents, etc. It is through such collaboration that the preparation of middle level teachers will also be realized. The key parties that must be involved in this effort are colleges and universities, state departments of education, NCATE, middle school state associations, and NMSA.

One need only look at the middle level teacher education programs featured in this monograph to see that many colleges and universities have already accepted the challenge to lead efforts to further middle level teacher education. Too often higher education waits until the demand filters down (up) before taking action. We can no longer afford to do this. Teacher education is too complex to approach in such a linear fashion. The demand for teachers prepared and qualified to teach young adolescents must involve a coordinated attack from several fronts at the same time. We can no longer wait while a part of our arsenal does battle before we enter the skirmish. Neither can we afford not to coordinate our efforts, and even worse, we cannot afford to fight among ourselves, for surely the battle will be lost and the casualties will be the young adolescents in our middle schools.

This monograph is intended to help stimulate further collaboration by sharing what colleges and universities have already done in efforts to pioneer middle level teacher education in their respective states. In addition, we hope this sense of collaboration will spread to other higher education institutions who currently do not have programs and encourage them to begin looking at how they might prepare teachers to work with young adolescents.■

2. NMSA–Leader in Middle Level Teacher Education

The new National Middle School Association position paper, *This We Believe: Developmentally Responsive Middle Level Schools* (1995) identified twelve needed characteristics. The very first one is "Educators committed to young adolescents," and in the elaboration this statement is included: "Educators need specific preparation before they enter middle level classrooms and continuous professional development as they pursue their careers" (p. 14).

The Professional Preparation and Certification Committee was one of the original standing committees established by NMSA. Members of this committee are appointed by the president for a three year term. The committee consists of nine members plus the folio coordinator and the NCATE board representative. Although the members of the committee generally represent higher education, representatives from state departments of education, teachers, administrators, and university students also serve as members. The committee has an annual budget which is approved by the board and meets once a year in addition to meeting at the annual conference and communicating by phone, FAX, and mail between meetings. The committee has focused its efforts primarily in the areas of professional forums, publications, and as a constituent member of NCATE.

Professional Forums

The committee's sole purpose is to work toward the stated goal of the association – to assure that quality educators work with young adolescents in our middle schools. Historically, one of the primary means by which the committee carries out this charge is through offering focused sessions at the annual conferences. These sessions provide forums through which issues related to the professional preparation of middle level teachers may be debated and discussed. During the last few years there has been an increasing demand for not only more sessions on teacher preparation at the annual conference, but sessions that go beyond merely discussing and debating, ones that deal with substantive solutions. The annual conference now has an entire strand devoted specifically to the professional preparation of middle level educators. The Professional Preparation and Certification Committee sponsors several of these sessions as well as a pre-conference workshop for teacher educators prior to the annual conference.

In addition to the annual conference, the Professional Preparation and Certification Committee has held other regional conferences in which middle level teacher educators have been invited to attend, share their programs, and discuss issues related to middle level teacher education. As a result of these conferences and the sessions at the annual conference, the committee has established a network designed to promote dialogue between and among middle level teacher educators across the nation. To further facilitate this interchange, the committee has published a directory of middle level teacher education programs in the United States (NMSA, 1992).

Publications

Another area in which the Professional Preparation and Certification Committee has worked to further middle level teacher education is in the area of publications. Although there has been a long-acknowledged need for qualified middle level teachers, it has only been recently that there has been anything substantive written regarding this need. In the 1980s, the Professional Preparation and Certification Committee sponsored some of the first writings addressing the need for middle level teacher education. In the 1990s NMSA has dramatically increased the number of publications on middle level teaher education in response to the increased interest in this area.

The following are publications dealing with middle level certification and professional preparation that have been published in the last three years. Although many of them can be directly linked to NMSA, some were written by authors not directly affiliated with NMSA or the publication itself was sponsored by agencies other than NMSA. However, each publication cited below has contributed to a better understanding of the issues and need for certification and professional preparation of teachers of young adolescents.

The following four documents were described briefly in Chapter One: *National Middle School Association/National Council for Accreditation of Teacher Education - Approved Curriculum Guidelines* (1991), *National Association of State Directors of Teacher Education and Certification Outcomes-Based Standards and Portfolio Assessment* (1993), *Turning Points: Preparing Youth for the Twenty-first Century* (1989), and *Model Standards for Beginning Teacher Licensing and Development: A Resource for State Dialogue* (1992).

- *Professional Certification and Preparation for the Middle Level: A Position Paper of the National Middle School Association* (1991). This NMSA position paper on middle level professional preparation and certification is based on the position statement first written in 1980 and revised in 1986. The Professional Preparation and Certification Committee was responsible for the position statement.

- *On Site: Preparing Middle Level Teachers Through Field Experiences* by Deborah A Butler, Mary A. Davies, and Thomas S. Dickinson (1991). The importance of early and continuous field experience in the preparation of middle level teachers is highlighted in this book. The roles of the university and the public school in providing a meaningful experience for prospective teachers are well delineated by the authors.

- *Windows of Opportunity: Improving Middle Grades Teacher Education* by Peter Scales (1992). This publication reported the findings from a national study sponsored by the Dewitt Wallace-Readers Digest Foundation which investigated and made recommendations for improving the preparation of middle level teachers. Although these findings were not encouraging regarding the current status of middle level teacher education, the study did indicate that we need to take immediate advantage of the windows of opportunity which now exist to improve middle level teacher preparation.

- *The Early Adolescence/Generalist and Early Adolescence/English Language Arts Standards,* National Board for Professional Teaching Standards (1992). The NBPTS is in the process of developing advanced certification standards for teachers currently in the field. The first two areas which were selected by the National Board for the development of standards were middle school generalist and middle school English/language arts. These two sets of standards will eventually be used to assess knowledge and skills of middle level teaching for those seeking advanced certification in these two areas. Eighty-one teachers comprised the first wave of teachers achieving this distinction.

- *Growing Pains: The Making of America's Middle Level Teachers,* by Peter C. Scales and C. Kenneth McEwin (1994). This study looks at middle level teacher preparation from a somewhat different perspective. Rather than looking at teacher preparation programs, this study surveyed 2139 middle level teachers about their professional preparation. From the data collected, recommendations were made to improve the preparation of middle level teachers based not only on the lack of preparation cited by the teachers, but also on the teaching qualities they saw as important as revealed in their own experiences.

- *The Professional Preparation of Middle Level Teachers: Profiles of Successful Programs,* by C. Kenneth McEwin and Thomas S. Dickinson (1995). This substantial book features descriptions of 14 different middle level teacher preparation programs throughout the nation. Examples of undergraduate as well as graduate programs are cited. The authors have selected a variety of different programs from higher education institutions that are large-small, private-public, and campus based-field based. Generalizations and recommendations included.

- "Reforming Middle Grades Teacher Preparation," edited by Thomas O. Erb (1995). This themed issue of the *Middle School Journal* contains nine articles that describe the latest attempts to reform middle grades teacher education through collaborative efforts between middle schools and teacher education institutions.

- *A Vision of Excellence: Organizing Principals for Middle Grades Teacher Preparation,* by C. Kenneth McEwin, Thomas S. Dickinson, Thomas O. Erb, and Peter C. Scales (1995). The authors first give the reader a brief history of middle grades teacher education as a prelude to presenting a conceptual foundation for the preparation of teachers for the middle grades. This monograph not only address the competencies needed for teaching at the middle grades, but more importantly presents a clearly stated framework for middle grades teacher education programs.

NMSA Joint Relationship with NCATE

Not only has NMSA published extensive materials that advocate the preparation and certification of middle level teachers and provided forums where issues and successful practices can be shared, the association has also been involved in determining policies that affect teacher education itself. In 1987, the NMSA Board of Trustees approved joining NCATE to become one of 28 constituent members. By doing so, NMSA was recognized as the only national professional organization that could establish middle level teacher preparation guidelines and assess NCATE accredited institutions that have middle level teacher education programs. The following year the Professional Preparation and Certification Committee wrote the middle level teacher preparation guidelines and in 1989 submitted them for NCATE approval. The Advanced Guidelines, which included guidelines for the masters, specialist, and doctoral levels, were approved in 1990.

As the professional association with sole authority to assess middle level teacher preparation programs in NCATE-affiliated higher education institutions, NMSA now has a means of directly affecting the quality of middle level teacher preparation. This is a responsibility that NMSA has taken very seriously. It has established a folio review system that involves 15 different educators who have been screened, selected from a national pool of applicants, and trained for this task. These 15 reviewers work in teams of three to evaluate each program submitted. It is not unusual for the reviewers to reject a program on first reading. However, many of these programs are able to pass successfully after a rejoinder process has been completed and schools have addressed the concerns the folio reviewers raised. The guidelines themselves have provided assistance to schools wishing to establish middle level teacher preparation programs, while the folio process has given NMSA a unique opportunity to monitor the quality of existing programs.

As a constituent member of NCATE, NMSA has recently been afforded an additional opportunity to impact middle level licensure and certification. NCATE's State Partnership Program permits a state to enter into a partnership wherein both NCATE and the state jointly share responsibility for accrediting teacher education programs. In essence, this means that the state guidelines and the NCATE guidelines have been found compatible, allowing teacher education programs within the state to be assessed through a jointly agreed upon process. The significance of the state partnership to NMSA is the fact that the association is involved in the approval process of the state guidelines. Before a state is granted state partnership status, each of the associations who are NCATE constituent members evaluate the state standards which apply to their association to assess whether the state standards comply with the association guidelines. This has given NMSA the opportunity to assess several state middle level certification/licensure standards, many of which have fallen far short of being equivalent to the NMSA/NCATE guidelines. However, the chance to assess state middle level certification/ licensure standards is a big step toward assuring that states recognize the importance of developing appropriate certification/ licensure standards for middle level teachers.

It is clear that NMSA has played a major role, perhaps the leading role, in efforts to ensure that our middle schools are staffed with teachers who are knowledgeable about and committed to the education of young adolescents. The NMSA/NCATE middle level teacher education guidelines reflect the collective statement of the positions held by NMSA regarding middle level teacher preparation. ■

3. *Exemplary Practices*

This chapter features elements from undergraduate and graduate middle level teacher preparation programs that effectively address a specific standard in the NMSA/NCATE guidelines. It is hoped that the descriptions contained in this chapter will serve as a stimulus and provide direction to institutions seeking to improve their middle level teacher education programs.

The text follows the sequence and format of the original *National Middle School Association/National Council for Accreditation of Teacher Education - Approved Curriculum Guidelines.* The chapter begins with the Basic Program for preservice teacher preparation. The subsequent sections address masters, 5th year, specialist and doctoral programs. Each guideline is stated, followed by a brief narrative which interprets the guideline; then at least two examples describing how specific institutions have addressed that particular guideline are provided. As this chapter makes clear, there are many ways of meeting the guideline, but the essence of a particular guideline is always addressed.

Undergraduate

1.1 An identifiable program is established for prospective middle level teachers.

Having a well-defined knowledge base is one of the criteria for NCATE accreditation. Likewise, it is important for middle level teacher education programs to have well-defined knowledge bases. While listing courses from a catalog provides some evidence of the existence of a middle level teacher education program, it is not likely to reveal the underlying essence of a program. A well-conceived knowledge base provides a common foundation which binds courses together into a cohesive teacher education program designed to prepare teachers to work with young adolescents.

University of Georgia

Curriculum and instruction for young adolescents should be based on their developmental needs. Thus, creating an appropriate match between the schools young adolescents attend and their developmental needs is central to the philosophy that informs the B.S. Ed. program in Middle School Education at the University of Georgia.

In terms of cognitive, physical, social, personal, and moral development, students in the middle grades undergo more change than at any other time of their lives except infancy. Additionally, the middle grades are particularly critical for female students, students from minority cultures, and students of low socioeconomic status. It is during these years that they form attitudes about the relevance of school and academic activities for their future. During these years, they also make decisions about how long to remain in school and whether or not to prepare for higher education. Thus, it is important that middle school teachers and administrators design curriculum and instruction so that all students can reach their full potential. The undergraduate middle school education program at the University of Georgia is designed to achieve this goal.

Key components of the program that bind courses together to achieve this goal include: 1) in-depth study of young adolescent development and the implications for middle school teachers, 2) content and methods courses designed exclusively for prospective middle school teachers, and 3) integrated content and methods courses designed and team-taught so students take content area courses (e.g., biology) while simultaneously taking methods courses to learn how to teach that content to middle school students.

Western Kentucky University

Institutional leadership, beginning with the president's office, values a responsive program reflective of ongoing educational reform on a state and national basis. Program documentation recognizes the young adolescent's self-worth as the central focus. Next, the conceptualization expands to identify and include the young adolescent's social, academic, and intellectual development needs. Finally, academic expectations for middle level teachers, consistent with underlying beliefs, are identified along with performance outcomes and assessment measures. Teacher education, psychology, and content area faculty work hand-in-hand to update and implement a strong research-based program for prospective middle level teachers, grades 5-8, reflective of the conceptual knowledge base.

2.1 Understanding the physical, social, emotional, intellectual, and moral development of early adolescents in various social contexts.

One of the primary goals of middle level teacher education is to help prospective teachers facilitate the growth and development of young adolescents. It is thus critical that middle level teacher education provide a thorough understanding of the developmental nature and needs of young adolescents.

University of North Carolina at Greensboro

The primary goal of the Middle Grades Education Program at UNC Greensboro is to foster inquiry into the needs of middle level students and ways teachers can meet those needs. Our philosophical orientation is "teacher as inquirer," a stance that places us in the "inquiry-oriented paradigm" of teacher education. Inquiry-oriented perspectives emphasize the development of capacities for "reflective action" (Dewey, 1933), an ongoing process of examining issues embedded in thinking and practice. The goal of an inquiry-oriented program is to prepare teachers who can reflect on the origins, purposes, and consequences of their actions.

Understanding the unique developmental needs of young adolescents is the central theme of our professional courses. Students begin their professional course work with CUI 202, Human Development, which provides a strong foundation in biological and psychological development. This foundation is extended with clinical experiences that take place in their sophomore year in conjunction with CUI 250, Teaching as a Profession. As students begin working together in the Middle Grades Inquiry Team at the beginning of their junior year, their studies are organized around the hallmarks of "an enlightened middle-level perspective." The unique needs of students and teachers are highlighted, and critical issues such as "grouping" and "teaming" are explored. Inquiry Seminars (CUI 350, 375, 400), taken across the junior and senior years, provide a series of opportunities to observe students, conduct interviews, and explore developmental issues first-hand. CUI 335, Integrated Reading Instruction, provides an introduction to the process of assessing the needs and interests of young adolescents as the basis of teaching. We then address middle level philosophies and basic principles of curriculum addressed in CUI 442, Teaching and Learning in the Middle Grades.

The developmental needs of young adolescents are underscored in the study of philosophy and curriculum. Developmentally appropriate instructional strategies are emphasized in all of the methods courses. Structured seminars during student teaching provide an opportunity to synthesize their insights on the developmental appropriateness of school practices and to generate strategies for enhancing success for all students.

Webster University

Although Standard 2.1 is addressed throughout the Webster University middle school teacher preparation program, the topic of early adolescent development is primarily discussed in SSC 554.01, Psychology of Early Adolescence.

The course is introduced with the viewing of Rob Reiner's film *Stand By Me.* This film illustrates in humorous and dramatic ways the search for identity and understanding in four twelve year old boys living in a small town in Oregon. The boys differ in their levels of physical, social, and cognitive maturity, yet they have bonded together in friendship and in the search for the body of a dead classmate.

Cognitive development in early adolescence is taught primarily through the theories of Piaget (1972) and Elkind (1967, 1994). Students test out the theories with Piagetian experiments. Early adolescent girls' difficulties with math and science are studied from a cross-cultural perspective. Other topics include the nature of "goofing off" in schools, entropic states in the classroom, and the theory of multiple intelligences.

Puberty, the psychological significance of pubertal change, and identity formation are studied from a cross-cultural perspective. Students have opportunities to conduct small scale studies about menarche, rites of passage, views of self, ethnic identity, gender role identity, and moral reasoning.

Important social relationships for young adolescents include the peer group and relationships with adults such as parents, teachers, and advisors. Students learn about these relationships through observations, interviews, and reading current research studies. Adolescents are observed in their "natural habitats" including classrooms, malls, and amusement parks.

A Portrait of Young Adolescents in the 1990s (Scales, 1991) provides information about current trends and issues for young adolescents including health concerns, sexual activity, family change, criminology, and poverty.

2.2   Plan the teaching/learning process to facilitate early adolescent development.

Middle level teacher education must go beyond just helping the prospective teacher understand the developmental needs and characteristics of young adolescents. It must also provide opportunities for prospective teachers to apply this knowledge to their own beliefs about the teaching/learning process.

Central Michigan University

The new Middle Level Education minor, part of the B.S. Ed. program for elementary certification candidates at Central Michigan University, emphasizes classroom-based theories applied to field-based practice for prospective middle level teachers to strengthen their knowledge of the developmental needs and characteristics of young adolescents and the subsequent development of appropriate strategies for the teaching and learning process.

The total middle level education minor is based on the NMSA/NCATE basic guidelines and focuses continually on the issues of early adolescent development. The program includes required course work on the principles of middle level education, middle level teaching methodology and materials, teaching culturally diverse students, dynamics of interpersonal communications, and interdisciplinary processes and strategies in teaching reading, writing, thinking, and learning. These courses are complemented by a required field experience taken concurrently with the methods course. A strong emphasis in this program is taking theory and research and applying it to practice in a middle level school and classroom where we focus on preadolescents and their developmental needs. Middle level courses begin with the developmental issues of preadolescence.

Learner expectations include visiting several middle level schools to identify and evaluate programs based on meeting the needs of young adolescents, designing a middle level curriculum for a team based on Alexander's Curriculum Model, designing a "service learning" project for young adolescents to enhance school-community collaboration, and preparing a change proposal for team teaching or an advisor-advisee program appropriate for meeting the needs of young adolescents. In addition, during the methods course, future middle level teachers are expected to prepare a team-planned thematic unit of study based on personal and social concerns of young adolescents addressing James Beane's curriculum proposals. These thematic units involve preadolescents in the planning process, are outcome-based, and include authentic assessment opportunities. This expectation will be enhanced for future teachers through a curriculum component of the Michigan Schools in the Middle Project at Central Michigan University funded by the W.K. Kellogg Foundation and permit students to utilize the vast resources of the project's Center for Excellence in Middle Level Education.

Perhaps the most appropriate opportunity is the mid-tier field practicum in a middle level school identified by CMU's Middle Level Teacher Preparation Committee as meeting specific middle level education criteria. During this experience, future teachers will be able to observe and analyze young adolescent behavior and actions reflective of their developmental needs. They then formulate descriptions of the role and function of middle level team members, exploratory teachers, and advisors based on meeting the needs of preadolescents. It is expected that these teacher preparation components will encourage new middle level teachers to begin a lifetime of reflection about their teaching and student learning based on developmental needs of young adolescents.

University of Georgia

The B.S. Ed. program in Middle School Education at the University of Georgia provides numerous and varied opportunities for prospective teachers to apply their knowledge of the developmental needs and characteristics of young adolescents to their own beliefs about the teaching and learning process.

First, in addition to in-depth study of young adolescent development, students in the program take content and methods courses designed exclusively for prospective middle school teachers. The content, activities, and assignments in these courses are structured to help students integrate and apply their knowledge of young adolescent development to the ways in which teaching and learning in the content areas (i.e., language arts, mathematics, science, and social science) can best take place in middle schools. A number of these courses have been co-developed and are team taught by arts and sciences faculty and education faculty. For example, prospective middle school students in the program who have a major or minor area of study in science take a chemistry course and a teaching of chemistry course. These two courses are team taught in a block by an arts and science faculty member and an education faculty member. The content, activities, and assignments in the two courses are integrated so that the students in the courses learn chemistry while simultaneously learning the best and most appropriate ways to teach chemistry to middle school students.

Second, throughout the program, students are involved in extensive field experiences designed to help them apply their knowledge of young adolescent development to the teaching and learning that occurs in middle schools. Unique aspects of the University of Georgia field experiences include placements in a variety of settings (e.g., rural, suburban) so that the prospective teachers in the program have experiences with students from different backgrounds, cultures, and socioeconomic status. The diverse nature of the field experience placements provides the prospective teachers in the program with opportunities to examine their own beliefs about the teaching and learning process and how it applies to young adolescents.

2.3   Create and maintain a developmentally responsive program and learning environment.

Middle level teacher education must enable prospective teachers to transfer their knowledge of the growth and development of young adolescents into ways and means of creating a classroom climate that is not only developmentally appropriate, but also provides young adolescents with a safe and caring environment in which to learn.

Illinois State University

As effective middle level teachers seek to engage middle level students in active hands-on experiences, the ISU middle level teacher training program strives to engage teacher candidates in skill development and practice that promote firsthand knowledge of learner characteristics and needs. These skills are practiced in both the classroom and the field-based setting.

In the first middle school methods course, Education and the Early Adolescent, students participate in exercises that ask students to blend facts about middle level learners with useful instructional techniques. In concert with this synthesis activity, students participate in focused observations in a middle school guided by observation instruments that emphasize the unique characteristics of the middle level learner.

In the advanced methods course, Junior High/Middle School Curriculum, students conduct interviews with middle school teachers and parents. This assignment is designed to give teacher candidates insight into the educational needs of the middle level learner, while providing early experience in talking with parents about their child's needs.

In the clinical setting, one activity available to students is working in an advisory program at the laboratory school. Students prepare activities with their peers, meet with the school faculty and counseling staff, and spend one advisory period each month with a student group. During a portfolio assignment, teacher candidates shadow a middle level learner, and interview teachers in grades before and after their assigned level. "Hands-on" experience is the goal.

Utah State University

To accomplish Standard 2.3, elementary education majors at Utah State University are immersed in a five level, field based program preparing them to teach grades 1-8. The five levels correspond to the acronym SODIA (self, others, disciplines, implementation, application), and all levels emphasize the following strands: assessment, classroom management, curriculum, effective teaching, learner, parent and community, diversity, personal and professional development.

All SODIA levels stress an understanding of the growth and development of 6 to 14 year olds, along with the application of that understanding through "hands-on" experience. Students work alongside classroom teachers as they create an age appropriate, child centered curriculum, design and deliver developmentally responsive instruction, and implement management techniques that empower children to live in a democratic society. To accomplish this, all students go through the following sequence:

1. Level I (self): Completion of a 3 credit orientation course which explores the world of teaching, complete with 10 hours of observation at various grade levels.

2. Level II (others): Completion of a 15 credit block in Foundational Studies in Teaching Middle Level, Education of the Exceptional Child, Educational Psychology, and Practicum in Elementary/Middle Education. Level II students complete a 20 day practicum in one of four areas: early childhood, elementary, middle, or service learning. During the practicum, students work alongside regular classroom teachers (in the service learning option, students work with community social agencies) two days each week, while learning about growth and development of young adolescents.

3. Level III (disciplines): Completion of a 15 credit block of classroom and seminar experiences at the Edith Bowen Laboratory School, planning and delivering interdisciplinary content in the "methods" areas of reading, social studies, language arts, and mathematics.

4. Level IV (implementation): Completion of the student teaching experience at two different grade levels, one of which must be 6-8 for students pursuing middle education, along with the student teaching seminar that focuses on the middle grades.

5. Level V (application): Graduates of the program transition into the profession of teaching. Informal collaboration between the university and employing school districts is maintained as well as follow-up surveys to evaluate the total program.

3.1 Articulate and apply a sound philosophy of middle level education.

Middle level teacher education must not only provide prospective teachers with a sound philosophical foundation of middle level education, but must also give them opportunities to internalize and articulate these basic concepts. In order to be an effective teacher, one must not only have a knowledge of teaching, but also be able to take that knowledge and develop a belief system upon which he/she can act.

Elizabeth City State University

The foundation for the middle school program is addressed extensively in Foundations of Education. This course covers a review of the nature of the students who are generally enrolled in grades 6 through 9. The course is also designed to provide an overview of the historical, social, and cultural influences in the development of the middle school concept. An in-depth study of the philosophy, organization, administration, and curriculum is provided.

Students not only learn about the philosophical foundation of middle school, they are also given the opportunity to see how this philosophy is put into action in the classroom. Initially, students are assigned to teams of two to four persons depending on the composition of the class. Each academic area is represented on a team. After instruction in process and procedures of functioning within a team; advisory (teacher based guidance); cooperative learning; exploratory curriculum; individualized learning; and the nature of the curriculum in each area, as outlined in the North Carolina Course of Basic Study, each student creates authentic products for each section.

Each student collaborates within his/her team in designing an integrated unit utilizing basic academic subjects, drama, movement, art, and music. An appropriate team bulletin board is designed and produced by the team. Each student designs a teacher based advisory unit and simulates one session for the entire class. Each student selects an appropriate lesson and designs a cooperative learning lesson. The students design an exploratory unit created around the unique skills of the individual students in the class. They are required to produce a file with a minimum of 100 innovative ideas that can be utilized in the middle grades program. The students are required to observe in a public middle school for a minimum of 20 hours and discuss practices in relation to theory.

Competencies and skills addressed in the foundations course are refined and reinforced in all other middle grades courses.

University of North Carolina at Wilmington

The principles on which middle school education rests are studied and discussed in our first course in the middle school sequence, Middle School Programs and Practices. During this same semester, the students observe and teach in advisor/advisee homebase settings in local middle schools. Toward the end of the semester, the students spend time in class writing answers to a series of questions using a "forced-writing" teaching strategy. This leads to the generation of a philosophy of middle level education. Answers are discussed in groups, organized, peer edited and put away for safe keeping. During the apprenticeship of the methods courses, students are asked to keep reflective logs of field experiences and comment on their philosophy as it compares with and is influenced by the practices they observe. At the end of the semester a portfolio of justified selections is presented at a celebration of learning attended by students and instructors across the four methods courses. At the beginning of the internship semester, a polished, edited, correct, one page philosophy of education is submitted. In this manner, we feel that our students reach the public schools able to articulate and act upon a consistent system of beliefs.

3.2   Apply an understanding of the organizational structure appropriate for middle level learners (such as: interdisciplinary teaming, block-time, cross grade grouping).

Organizational structures for middle level schools are becoming uniquely different than those found in elementary or high school. It is critical that prospective teachers in middle level teacher education programs have a working knowledge of which organizational structures are appropriate for the education of young adolescents and why.

East Carolina University

The program at ECU offers students several opportunities to explore the nature of the middle school structure and organization. Students are exposed in MIDG 2123 to actually visiting schools with teaming and a variety of schedules and student arrangements (although the latter is not as frequently actually used). In MIDG 3001 the students have an opportunity to explore the nature of the middle school young adolescent and a variety of curricula and instructional arrangements suitable for the age group. Part of this experience is a set of assignments: readings, analytic observation reports, role playing, simulations, etc., that provide students with both a theoretical as well as a practical exposure to alternative patterns of school, class and student organization. These types of assignments are re-enforced in successive courses and practicum experiences, for example, building curriculum units as an interdisciplinary team; and organizing year-long, long-range, and unit length integrative curriculum and instructional experiences. To reinforce the constructivist approach, the curriculum also stresses authentic assessment.

Western Kentucky University

Students are assigned to four member interdisciplinary teams. These teams work together to conceptualize and develop integrated instructional units and assist teaching teams in area schools (each individual team member must work in an assigned middle school for 75 contact hours prior to student teaching). In addition, students must design action plans providing alternative scheduling techniques that promote successful development of the young adolescent's self-worth. Diverse student needs are investigated through required sociograms and case studies in actual classroom situations. Non-graded and cross-age grouping strategies are thoroughly explored in area schools as well as research based techniques to account for diverse student needs. Program performance assessment criteria require that undergraduates teach early adolescents and provide videotapes in order to demonstrate understandings. Educational reform efforts in Kentucky reflect and support organizational plans based on students' needs at all levels of academic development (P-12); therefore, real-world examples of block scheduling and cross-age grouping are readily available for undergraduate experiences.

3.3 Understand and implement a balanced and integrated middle level curriculum which includes: (1) skills for con-

tinued learning, (2) organization of knowledge, (3) exploratory/ enrichment opportunities, and (4) teacher based guidance.

Curriculum is a complex mixture of many variables. However, a balance among these various aspects of curriculum has always been a priority when developing middle level curriculum. Middle level teacher education must help prospective teachers understand how these various components of middle level curriculum interrelate in such a way as to provide an educational environment that is developmentally appropriate for young adolescents.

Elizabeth City State University

In addition to the activities described in standard 3.1, a course in guidance is required for all middle grades students. They observe in a public middle grades school for a minimum of 20 hours. They produce a plan for a total teacher-based guidance program. They must include research concerning the psychological and physiological attributes of the middle school student that would necessitate the need for an advisory program. They observe and note instances of those attributes. They are especially observing for that "advisory moment" which is included in their plan. The advisory plan includes activities for orientation to new schools and new situations; personal growth; decision making; career exploration; learning to live; uniqueness of self; appreciation for others; interpersonal relationships; planning and organization; dealing with emotions; being health wise; legal and moral rights for self and others; and peer help activities. Students may utilize "canned" activities," but they must be tailored to meet the needs of the students being served.

A variety of conferences and workshops are offered which faculty and students attend. Copies of the *Middle School Journal,* North

Carolina Middle School Association materials, and other current resources are utilized to enhance instruction, help students remain current and learn about innovations for the middle school.

St. Cloud University

Education 437 (Schools for Early Adolescents) and Education 438 (Education of the Emerging Adolescent) provide in-depth coverage of the rationale and practice for interdisciplinary planning, exploratory programs, and teacher-based guidance (advisor-advisee) programs. Early Adolescent Block students work in teams to plan an interdisciplinary unit, exploratory options, and advisor-advisee activities. All of these planned activities are implemented in the practicum experience to the extent that they can be integrated into a cooperating teachers' plans.

3.4 Understand the interrelationship among the fields of knowledge.

Middle level teacher education must provide prospective teachers with a foundation of the content areas without narrowly specializing them in one particular area. Equally as important, middle level teacher education must help prospective teachers understand ways and means of integrating these fields of knowledge in a meaningful and organized manner (parallel planning, correlated teaching, interdisciplinary education, integrated instruction).

East Carolina University

Students in the middle grades program are required to have two concentrations from science, mathematics, social studies or language arts as prescribed by state certification. In all courses, students are encouraged to see the relationship of their concentrations within their own program, but also among all concentrations. In order to assure student recognition of this interrelationship, conceptual learning is emphasized, and curriculum and instructional materials are required to be interdisciplinary, and, where possible, integrative in nature. Emphasis on teaming and team planning; unitary structures which are built around themes or topics; and modeling of interdisciplinary planning and instruction by course instructors are all utilized in the ECU program. Attempts are also being made to provide an umbrella concept to accumulated student knowledge from their general education background – which is often overlooked by the liberal arts programs.

University of Northern Iowa

The Middle/Junior High Education major at UNI offers two courses, Middle/Junior High School Curriculum (210) and Language Arts Across the Curriculum (230), which focus on cross-curricular connections. The M/JHS Curriculum course (210) includes an overview of all subject areas, exploratory elements, and enrichment opportunities. Students are introduced to various models of curriculum integration and develop strategies to implement an integrated curriculum. Micro-teaching and the development of cross-curricular thematic units provide opportunities for the students to observe, explore, design, and demonstrate their understanding about the various fields of knowledge and ways of knowing.

The Language Arts Across the Curriculum course is designed to prepare teachers to teach in ways that allow young adolescents to use language as a tool for learning across the curriculum. Reading, writing, speaking, and listening are viewed as integrated processes and as the basic tools through which young adolescents learn. Particular emphasis is given to learning specific teaching strategies which guide young adolescents' use of reading and writing to learn in content subjects.

3.5 Adapt curriculum and instruction to the learning patterns of each student.

Prospective teachers in middle level teacher education programs must be able to apply knowledge of middle level curriculum and instruction to the learning patterns of young adolescents. In order to effectively accomplish the task, they must be able to identify the various levels of cognitive development as well as the different modalities of learning exhibited by young adolescents.

Central Michigan University

The new Middle Level Education minor, part of the B.S.Ed. program for elementary certification candidates at Central Michigan University, encourages future middle level teachers to review issues, theories, and research related to appropriate middle level curriculum and instruction. A first course on principles of middle level education includes the topics of team teaching strategies, Alexander's curriculum model, thematic units, interdisciplinary teaching, James Beane's curriculum model, and curriculum implications for preadolescents related to the newly proposed Michigan Core Curriculum.

Then, future middle level teachers are involved in an entire course focusing on middle level teaching methodologies and materials based on preadolescent needs and curriculum models. While theories and appropriate practices are considered, the total program constantly examines ways of providing success for all students: success individually, in small groups, and on larger teams, based on the physical, social, emotional, and intellectual developmental needs of preadolescents.

Future teachers consider flexible scheduling, small group work, cross-age grouping, cooperative learning, outcomes-based education, mastery learning, self-esteem, exploration, and advisor-advisee programs, as well as knowledge related to dimensions of learning and learning styles and theories embodied in *Bloom's Cognitive Taxonomy, Krathwohl's Affective Taxonomy* or *Williams' Creative Taxonomy.* Also dealt with are instructional tools such as gaming and simulations, learning centers, investigation task cards, case studies, study kits, and learning activity packs, all of which will enhance their knowledge base as learner-centered teachers. This program, as well as other Central Michigan University Teacher Education programs, focuses on a CLEAR model for teacher preparation: "C"=Content and knowledge-driven; "LEA"=Learner-centered; and "R"=Reflective practice in relevant and diverse settings.

These issues led us to support a major curriculum component in the Michigan Schools in the Middle Project funded by the W.K. Kellogg Foundation at Central Michigan University based on thematic instruction considering Beane's proposals related to personal and social concerns of preadolescents. Involving all students in planning questions and realistic, relevant instructional activities presents opportunities for student choices. Authentic assessment and many performance-based culminating activities are included. With these opportunities, we expect our new middle level teachers to be prepared to focus on the learning patterns of each student and provide curriculum and instruction accordingly.

Illinois State University

Prospective middle level educators seem to learn well the lessons they live. In the spirit of immersion, ISU middle level teacher candidates develop materials and participate in clinical experiences focusing on the study and identification of cognitive development of middle level learners. Knowledge of learning styles is gained through experiences with self and peer analysis, students' observation, and learning group discussions.

In the middle level philosophy course, The Junior High/ Middle School, teacher candidates become absorbed in the examination of all of the important theories of early adolescent growth and development, e.g., Bloom, Piaget, Krathwohl, Kohlberg, etc. As a synthesizing activity, teacher candidates work cooperatively to plan a middle school project that is composed of building a theoretical framework for a middle school and then translating it into specific programs for middle level learners.

The middle school planning project not only requires recommendations for curriculum, teaching techniques, programs, and activities, but teams state a rationale for each component in the plan. At this point, groups draw upon their knowledge of work by Johnson and Johnson, Slavin, Kagan, and other advocates of cooperative learning; and they utilize their background in individualization of instruction from George, Walberg, Doda, and other established writers.

In a pre-student teaching 50 hour internship, ISU middle level teacher candidates classify learning styles through observation of early adolescents. Work by Grasha and Reichmann provide six student learning styles that guide teacher candidates' study prior to observations. The reports generate valuable reflection.

3.6 Facilitate students' personal growth through appropriate instructional procedures, relevant curriculum content, and supportive personal relationships.

Middle level teacher education must help prospective teachers organize and conduct their classes in such a way as to facilitate students' personal growth both through the content they teach and the interactions that take place within their classrooms.

North Georgia College

Appropriate instructional procedures and relevant curriculum content are first addressed during the teaching field/methods courses required of students during the content phase of their program. Further emphasis is given to these areas during the curriculum and methods and materials courses during the block phase. Students are introduced to the Quality Core Curriculum, Georgia's statewide mandated curriculum which specifies by grade level concepts and objectives to be addressed, and are expected to plan lessons which reflect appropriate levels of skills instruction according to the grade level they work with during their field experience as well as during their student teaching quarter.

Facilitating students' personal growth through supportive personal relationships is emphasized throughout a student's program of preparation. Students are initially introduced to the concept during the foundations phase of their program in the required Human Growth and Development, Introduction to Education, Educational Psychology, Introduction to Exceptional Children, and Nature and Development of the Middle Grades Learner courses. During the block phase of their program, middle grades majors study the research on characteristics of effective teachers, including interpersonal characteristics. Particular emphasis is given to supportive personal relationships during the classroom management course in which students learn strategies for managing the total instructional setting including grouping, teacher-student relationships, and coping with conflict. During both the block field experience and the student teaching quarter, students are required to demonstrate skill in establishing effective and supportive interpersonal relationships with their students. Further, during the initial teaching year, beginning teachers are evaluated three times in unannounced in-class observations. Using the Georgia Teacher Observation Instrument teachers have to demonstrate how they support students effectively.

Southwest Missouri State University

As part of a comprehensive middle school program at Southwest Missouri State University, both pre-service teachers and graduate students seeking certification complete a two-credit hour course, MID 525, Middle School Curriculum. Here, students learn how to develop, implement, and evaluate integrated curricula. Interdisciplinary thematic units that span advisory, exploratory, intramural, co-curricular, and required academic classes are designed to engage young adolescents in learning through real-life applications of relevant content. Students present their lessons for critique to career middle school teachers in simulated classroom settings. Video tapes of these teaching encounters are viewed by students for evaluation and subsequent refinement. Some units are developed collaboratively by pre-service, graduate, and career teachers who call on university/business/community partners and parent volunteers for assistance. These units are then field-tested in middle level classrooms. National, state, and local standards are incorporated into all curricular materials, and state assessments are identified as major instructional goals.

3.7 Foster active learning by employing a variety of classroom grouping patterns, including small group work and independent study.

Middle level teacher education must expose prospective teachers to a wide variety of teaching strategies and grouping techniques that can be effectively used with young adolescents. Middle school prospective teachers must also understand when and how to use these strategies/ techniques to best facilitate the learning taking place within the classroom.

Georgia Southern University

The undergraduate Middle Grades Program at Georgia Southern University is based on current research in middle level education. The program models central components of sound middle level education program for young adolescents (e.g., interdisciplinary team planning and instruction, teacher-based advisory, and exploration). Courses are clustered into five interdisciplinary blocks, each organized around an integrated curriculum. Faculty work as interdisciplinary teams, integrating the course content. Each interdisciplinary cluster includes sequential field experiences in grades five through eight. Course clusters integrate language arts, social studies, mathematics, science, and exploratory areas of art, music, and health/physical education. Students simulate interdisciplinary team planning and teaching in teams of two to four members. Developmentally appropriate teaching strategies and grouping patterns are integrated into each cluster. A central component is planning and teaching teacher-based advisory lessons, as well as integrating exploratory activities into the curriculum. Each student selects two areas of concentration from social studies, science, mathematics, language arts, art, music, or health/physical education (3.7). The program culminates with a full quarter of student teaching in a middle school classroom.

Barton College

The Middle School Teacher Certification program at Barton College begins with an introduction to the teaching profession which focuses on current educational issues, the history and philosophy of education, and educational terminology. Students write their own philosophy of education based on their understanding of past and present education.

Practicum students bridge the gap between the theoretical and practical by reflecting on administration, faculty, students, special needs, parental involvement and community resources. In methods class, students examine current issues, investigate best practice, analyze case studies, prepare interactive bulletin boards, and develop strategies for using 25 cooperative learning techniques. Apple and IBM CAI, gradebook, CD-ROM, and video disc programs are used as well as on-campus audio and video production facilities. Microteaching lessons provide practice using such techniques as set induction, closure, questioning skills, positive reinforcement, cooperative learning, stimulus variation, and authentic assessment.

Students in classroom management discuss the physical environment, time-on-task, independent practice, group work, working with parents, and increasing community involvement. During student teaching, students acquire and refine teaching skills while increasing self-awareness, confidence, and personal satisfaction in the real world of the professional educator.

3.8   Teach problem solving and communication skills (reading, listening, writing and speaking) as an integral part of all instruction.

Prospective middle level teachers must be prepared to assist young adolescents in acquiring skills which can be applied to all content fields. Thus they must be prepared to use the content within their teaching field(s) as a vehicle to reinforce and enhance these skills.

North Georgia College

Teaching problem solving and communication skills is emphasized during the content phase and the block phase of the program of preparation. Methods courses during the content phase (including language arts, mathematics, health and physical education, reading, science, and social studies) emphasize such areas as critical thinking skills, an inquiry approach to learning, and writing across the curriculum as integral parts of all instruction. The block phase requires students to plan for and implement problem solving strategies and communications skills in the lessons they plan in all areas of the curriculum. Additionally, students are expected to demonstrate skill in teaching problem solving and communications skills during both the block field experience and the student teaching quarter.

3.9 Perform guidance roles in formal and informal settings.

Teaching young adolescents requires more than merely presenting content. A prospective teacher must also be prepared to deal with the wide range of emotions that affect the young adolescent's behavior and performance in school. Middle level teacher education must provide prospective teachers with some basic guidance techniques that will enable them to recognize a student's problems, provide the student with support, and/or refer the student for further help.

Illinois State University

A commitment to the affective development of early adolescent learners is an essential component of effective middle schools. This statement has tremendous implications for middle level teacher preparation programs. At a time in their lives when most college students find early adolescence difficult to remember in their own experience, the ISU middle level teacher education program sharpens the focus through directed course activities and field-based experiences.

In the ISU middle level professional education sequence, each of the five middle level courses explores the topics of interpersonal communication skills and advisory activities in full class and group settings. Teacher candidates participate in advisory groups, and design original activities to use in their internships. Attention is also given to the affective development of the teacher candidate. The Myers-Briggs Type Indicator is administered to teacher candidates in Junior High/Middle School Curriculum. Getting to know oneself and how one relates to others is the goal of this activity.

Providing experiential activities in advisory topics can be a difficult task. The Metcalf Project has supplied the ISU program with an opportunity to engage teacher candidates in advisory time with middle level learners in the school setting. Monthly topics for sessions with students range from "getting to know you" activities to "gender respect" and "handling peer pressure." For teacher candidates, a new comfort level with advisory responsibilities and time spent with students developing a personal relationship has been invaluable.

University of Northern Iowa

Middle Level Socialization and Instruction (21M:135g) provides opportunities for teachers to develop instructional strategies and resources for meeting the developmental needs of young adolescents. Teachers examine in depth the characteristics of young adolescents and analyze the implications for instruction. Teachers learn to schedule advisor/advisee programs, create and present developmentally appropriate lessons, examine social concerns and their implications for middle level education, and examine their own roles as teachers and advisors.

3.10 Provide leadership for student activities.

Middle level teacher education should help prospective teachers realize the importance of interacting with young adolescents on both a formal and an informal basis. Prospective teachers have opportunities not only to observe, but also interact with young adolescents in classroom as well as in non-classroom environments.

University of Northern Colorado

One of the basic premises of middle level education is that young adolescents need to be involved in activities which are relevant to them. The same holds true in the preparation of teachers of young adolescents. At the University of Northern Colorado we have found the best way to help our students discover the benefits of involving their students in school-sponsored activities is to let them experience being involved in their own middle school student association. The University of Northern Colorado Association of Middle Level Education (UNCAMLE) is a student organization whose membership is comprised of primarily undergraduate students in the middle school teacher preparation program. However, a few full-time graduate students are members. They meet weekly and plan a variety of activities, including those of a professional nature and those that are purely social in nature. They have organized money raising projects to cover the cost of going to the NMSA conference as well as planned activities on campus in recognition of National Middle School Week. They have volunteered their services to work with schools in tutoring programs as well as assisting in sponsoring various middle school activities at local middle schools.

Through being a member of UNCAMLE, students have not only gained valuable experience in providing leadership for student activities, but they have also experienced the benefit of belonging to a group and the support one finds in participating in such a group. Through this experience it is hoped that transfer to their teaching will occur and they will realize how important involvement in school activities can be to young adolescents.

Ashland University

The formal association that middle grades teacher candidates experience occurs as part of the field experience programs. Ashland University places teacher candidates in four experiences that progress from basic observations and tutorial activities to the student teaching program. Providing opportunities for informal interactive involvement is somewhat more difficult to achieve. The forum and rationale for such experiences, however, is in place. Teacher candidates at Ashland University are encouraged and required to be involved in a variety of experiences with time commitments relative to the level of the field experience.

Ed. 130 provides opportunity for teacher education students to act in an informal manner with their tutorial group. Such socialization activities tend to happen in more depth as the level of field experiences evolves. In Ed. 330, which requires ten hours of field work per week, teacher education students often assist with coaching and advising duties and community involvement.

Teacher education students, and especially student teachers, are expected to involve themselves in the community beyond school hours. In some cases, the children in middle grades schools have the opportunity to attend activities on the AU campus.

3.11 Employ evaluation procedures appropriate to early adolescents.

Middle level teacher education must present a variety of techniques for assessing student progress. Prospective middle level teachers must also know how to assist students in evaluating their own progress as well as know effective ways to communicate with parents about their child's progress.

Ashland University

Middle level teacher education students are involved in a number of formal assessment evaluation programs and classes. All field experiences include seminars that provide learning experiences that teach middle level educators considerations and skills appropriate to the middle grades child. Ed. 130 is an early experience for teacher education students that allows for direct involvement in alternative assessments. For example, a good many of these assessment activities include personal interviews, narrative evaluations, and performance assessment.

The Middle Grades Education Certification program includes a particular course for evaluation and assessment. A range and variety of assessment and evaluation approaches and techniques are learned. In addition, students are taught documentation procedures as a phase of authentic assessment.

Middle level education students are expected to apply their assessment and evaluation learning to their teaching. The design of these experiences requires middle level teacher education students to review their procedures with their university supervisor and cooperating teacher. One phase of this process includes parents. During the Ed. 330 experience, middle level education students participate in parent teacher conferences for the purpose of assisting student academic and personal growth. This is a planned experience that is a component of the educational system in a number of middle schools in this area.

University of Northern Colorado

The need to know how to appropriately evaluate students

should be an important element of any teacher preparation program. Teachers are confronted with the task of evaluating students daily. Students in the University of Northern Colorado Middle School Teacher Preparation Program have an opportunity to look at the theory behind evaluation in several of their methods classes. They take a more specific look at how this theory directly applies to the young adolescent in their course entitled Instructional Practices in the Middle School.

In addition to studying various approaches for assessment and evaluation, the students also have an opportunity to observe alternative evaluation systems in use at the UNC Laboratory School. The Lab School does not use traditional grades but use portfolios. In many cases students are able to observe how this type of grading system plus the portfolios are used in parent conferences.

Another requirement of the UNC Teacher Education Program is that the student themselves develop a portfolio of their teacher education experience. Our goal in using portfolios is not only to help students assess their own program, but to also encourage them to use alternative methods such as portfolios with their own students.

3.12 Work collaboratively with teachers, staff members, parents, resource persons, and community groups.

In order for prospective middle level teachers to become productive and contributing members of a middle school, they need to learn how to work with the various constituencies associated with the school. Middle level teacher education must not only provide prospective teachers with the skills to assist them in being more collaborative, they must also provide opportunities to observe and participate in such interactions within the school setting.

Southwest Missouri Sate University

MID 539, The Middle School Teacher, a two-hour semester block course, may be taken for either graduate or undergraduate credit. In this class, students learn how to network with other teachers, parents, business and community leaders, universities, and other organizations to procure resources necessary for the implementation of innovative curricula and instructional approaches teaching and learning. While most of the networking takes place during face-to-face team planning times, FAX, voice mail, and other traditional methods are also used. Electronic communications (including distance learning via fiber-optics) is scheduled for use in the near future. Students observe video, make school site observations, conduct interviews, and collaborate with career teachers and administrators to identify instructional areas of concern for analysis.

Valdosta State University

The Department of Middle Grades Education (MGE) at Valdosta State University provides a collaborative training program, Reality 401, with public school faculties for three quarters. Reality 401 is a partnership among the MGE faculty, pre-service teachers and public school staffs, students, and parents.

Reality 401 begins with a workshop for the seniors in which they obtain their handbook, assignments, and program briefing. Mentors are also provided a handbook that includes guidelines for the program, evaluation forms, etc. During the first quarter of the senior year, students take three courses that are scheduled as a block. Curriculum in the Middle School, Language Arts Methods for Middle Grades and The Teaching of Developmental and Remedial Reading are taught by a three member college team. During this quarter the pre-service teachers become members of middle grades teams for 22 days. They are involved in all teacher duties through observing, participating, and teaching. The same procedure is followed the second quarter, which allows further modeling of team planning and teaching by the MGE faculty. During the second quarter, students take Social Studies Methods for Middle Grades, Mathematics Methods for Middle Grades and Science Methods for Middle Grades. Mentors and MGE supervisors evaluate pre-service teachers' professional and teaching abilities and make recommendations for improvement throughout each quarter. Reality 401 culminates with 10 weeks of student teaching during the third quarter. Seniors exit the program with 18 weeks of teaching experience.

The departmental plan is to immerse seniors in the middle school philosophy and practices in a true environment. Pre-service teachers are empowered to take charge of their education and development as a middle school teacher.

4.1 Teaching fields are broad, interdisciplinary, and encompass the major areas within those fields. Preparation in at least one field is required, but two different fields are preferred.

The content taught at the middle school level is intended to help young adolescents gain a breadth of knowledge and to see the interrelationships among various areas of knowledge. Likewise, the content preparation for prospective middle level teachers should include a breadth of content knowledge in at least one teaching field, if not more.

University of North Carolina Greensboro

Middle grades majors are required to take 45 semester hours of All University Liberal Education Requirements that include course work in composition, the humanities, natural sciences, social and behavioral sciences, and non-western cultures. They also complete a second major in one of eight academic disciplines such as English, Mathematics, or Biology and an additional concentration of 21-24 hours in a second teaching area. This provides for a total of at least 72 hours in general and specialty studies. The requirement for the Middle Grades Professional Core is 39 hours, including 12 hours of student teaching. Of the 126-129 hours required for the degree, one-third of the requirements are thus in professional courses, two-thirds are in general and specialty studies.

As indicated, middle grades majors are required to complete both a second major and an additional concentration of courses in a second teaching area. As a result, they complete a minimum of 21 hours in two of the four areas of certification (language arts, mathematics, science, and social studies). Requirements for each of these concentrations are broad and interdisciplinary. Students must also complete a methods course in each of their teaching areas. Methods courses provide systematic instruction in designing and evaluating strategies for teaching young adolescents.

University of Northern Iowa

The Middle School/Junior High School Education Major at the UNI is a dual major which must be combined with either an elementary or secondary teaching major. This major is designed to prepare students to teach pre- and young adolescents at the middle level (grades 4-9). Students complete General Education requirements, Professional Education requirements, the Middle School/Junior High requirements, major requirements for elementary or secondary teaching, and subject specialty requirements.

Thirty semester hours are required for the completion of the Middle School/Junior High School Major requirements. Fourteen of these hours are derived from a specific core of five classes with the remaining sixteen hours being electives which must include at least one methods course in the student's subject area or minor. The five required classes with descriptions follow:

200:116: Psychology of Adolescence (2 hours). Psychological concepts applied to adolescent intellectual, physical, and psychosocial behaviors; designed to improve understanding of, and relationships with, adolescents and their search for identity.

210:122: Classroom Management: Middle Level (3 hours). Classroom organization and behavior management compatible with the social/psychological characteristics of young adolescents.

210:135: Middle Level Socialization and Instruction (3 hours). Instructional strategies and resources for meeting the social/psychological personal needs of preadolescent and adolescent children within the classroom.

210:150: Middle School/Junior High School Curriculum (3 hours). Teaching methods, instructional resources, and school organization designed specifically for meeting the unique needs of the preadolescent and adolescent learner in both traditional junior high and middle school settings.

230:132: Language Arts Across the Curriculum (3 hours).

Emphasizes the role of language processes in learning and specific strategies to help elementary and secondary students gain concepts and develop abilities to learn through language processes in all subject areas.

4.2   When preparation in two fields is provided, those fields should be different (science and mathematics, for instance, not biology and chemistry).

Middle level curriculum has focused on the integration of knowledge rather than the categorization of knowledge into distinct content areas. If middle level prospective teachers have content preparation in more than one field of teaching, these fields should represent distinct teaching fields rather than content areas within the same teaching field. This will better enable the prospective teacher to teach in a more integrated fashion.

University of North Carolina Wilmington

All of our students are required to have a 24 hour concentration in one discipline as delineated by the corresponding academic department. That 24 hours may include related disciplines such as biology including six hours of chemistry. All students must also have a second teaching field in language arts, mathematics, science, or social studies selected from one of the three fields not covered by the academic concentration. Students must choose at least one course from each of the contributing disciplines or strands in these broad fields. In language arts we ask for a combination of literature, writing, linguistics, and communications. In mathematics, computer science and statistics as well as math courses are required. The needs of science teachers are covered with biology, chemistry, earth sciences, and physics classes and labs. And in social studies, students take not only history but the behavioral sciences of economics, geography, political science, and sociology or anthropology as well. In this manner we feel that our students have acquired both depth in one area and breadth across a broad field so that they are better able to contribute to integrated, multidisciplinary team teaching.

Valdosta State University

Middle Grades Education (MGE) majors at Valdosta State University develop a general knowledge base across four academics areas, humanities, mathematics and science, social studies, and courses appropriate for major. Once admitted to the teacher education program, preservice teachers must select two content areas in which to specialize. MGE majors are required to take 25 quarter hours of primary concentration courses and 20 quarter hours of secondary concentration courses. As their primary concentration, MGE majors may select language arts, mathematics, science, or social studies. For their secondary concentration they may select art, physical education, educational computing, foreign language, or one of the previous four.

Concentration courses are taught by the departments of Middle Grades Education, Vocational Education, Physical Education, along with the College of Arts and Sciences and the College of Fine Arts. For each of the concentration areas, the department has both required courses and electives. For example, individuals who select language arts as a concentration area are required to take both Advanced Grammar and Composition and Literature for Middle Grades Education. They then may select any three 300 or 400 level language arts courses to complete the primary concentration. An example of a secondary concentration is Educational Computing. In this area all courses are required. They are Introduction to Educational Computing, Introduction to Microprocessor Operations, Data Base Development, and Educational Authoring and Multimedia.

Besides the concentration areas, all MGE majors must take methods courses in the primary concentration areas: language arts, mathematics, science, and social studies. In these courses the integration of content and team planning is emphasized.

4.3 At least one methods course designed specifically for teaching at the middle level should be provided.

The nature and needs of young adolescents are uniquely different than the nature and needs of either younger children or older adolescents. Middle level teacher education must provide methods courses that focus on instructional strategies and classroom management techniques that meet the needs of young adolescents and are compatible with middle level curriculum.

Berry College

Middle grades pre-service teachers take two field-based courses during their junior year specifically focused on the middle grades. EDU 301W Middle Grades Curriculum involves in-depth study of the foundations of middle grades curriculum, including interdisciplinary units, middle-school concept, teaming, and developmental levels of students; writing lesson and unit plans for middle-grades; working with school personnel; and developing and applying teaching skills in a field-placement in a Professional Development Middle School. EDU 401 Middle-School Methods and Materials focuses on planning and instruction in middle school, classroom management, assessment, and educational media, along with applying teaching skills in a field-placement in a different Professional Development Middle School.

North Carolina State University

North Carolina is unique in that each of its 16 institutions in the state university system offers a dual concentration, university degree program in middle grades education, ex., the diploma says "middle grades education." (Also, the state has had specific middle grades certification since 1979; currently, certification is for grades 6-9, ninth grade being included to accommodate the few remaining junior high schools.) At North Carolina State University, students select teaching concentrations in either language arts/social studies education or math/science education, and take several methods courses in each concentration.

In the language arts/social studies concentration (housed in the Department of Curriculum and Instruction) students take ECI 307 Teaching Writing Across the Curriculum; GEO/ECI 200

Teaching Geography; ECI 430 Methods and Materials in Middle Grades Language Arts; and ECI 435 Methods and Materials in Middle Grades Social Studies. Some of the main emphases in these courses are the writing process and the reading/writing workshop approach, collaborative learning, and inquiry/discovery learning strategies.

In the math/science concentration (housed in the Department of Mathematics/Science Education), students take EMS 470 Methods of Teaching Math; EMS 474 Teaching Math in the Middle Years; and EMS 475 Methods of Teaching Science and Technology. Scientific discourse, laboratory technique and hands-on learning are some of the emphases in these courses.

In addition, students in both concentrations take other middle level courses which feature generic methods: ECI 203 or 205 Introduction to Teaching; ECI 310 Tutoring Adolescents; ECI 306 Reading in the Middle Years; ECI 415 Arts and Adolescence (using the arts as catalysts for content area and interdisciplinary teaching); and ECI 309 Teaching in the Middle Years. The first two are largely field based; the latter is taught with students placed in teams, culminating in the development of an interdisciplinary unit.

5.1 Early and continuing involvement in grades 5-9.

Middle level teacher education should allow prospective teachers to experience working with young adolescents throughout their teacher education program. These experiences should not only help prospective teachers better understand the developmental needs of young adolescents, but also begin to develop their beliefs about teaching as well as begin to recognize their strengths and weaknesses as teachers.

Georgia College

Georgia College provides prospective teachers experiences in working with young adolescents throughout their teacher education program. The program is two phased with off-campus programs emphasizing a fused, total day practicum experience and on-campus programs emphasizing an integrated set of practicums, correlated to course objectives and expected competency development. In both programs, students develop their beliefs about teaching through supervised in-field experiences in the course "Introduction to Education" and their first major sequence block course "The Educative Process." The off-campus students blend their experiences with a total day encounter at selected schools. On-campus programs integrate experience, with their normal course load, for a two (2) to five (5) week experience, ranging from two (2) hours per day to a total day experience.

University of North Carolina Greensboro

Middle grades majors begin their field experiences in CUI 250, Teaching as a Profession. Taken during the second semester of their sophomore year, CUI 250 requires students to spend one morning each week in a middle grades classroom. The focus of this first practicum is to explore the complexities of "life in classrooms." Assignments include a carefully sequenced series of classroom observations, interviews with teachers and students, tutoring, and small group instruction.

Classroom experiences grow more sophisticated as they join the Middle Grades inquiry team for their junior and senior year. Each team is assigned to a middle school site and works with university faculty and middle school teachers who serve as team leaders. Students spend ten hours in classrooms each week for the three semesters that precede student teaching. These practica provide opportunities to apply the theories and strategies learned in the methods courses that accompany them and to integrate instructional experiences. Progress is evaluated by intensive observation, discussion, and written reports. Seminars offered in conjunction with these internships provide many opportunities to analyze and evaluate experiences and examine middle level education in both local and global contexts.

5.2   Observation, participation, and teaching experiences ranging from individual to large group settings.

Middle level teacher education must help prospective teachers adapt to various educational settings within a middle school. Participating in a variety of settings within a school will allow prospective teachers to gain a more complete and comprehensive view of teaching at the middle level as both small group and large group sessions are common in middle schools.

West Georgia College

During the senior year block program, students are gradually immersed in a variety of field based experiences, ranging from observation to full-time teaching. During the fall quarter introductory block, students are placed in simulated settings (micro teaching) and spend some time involved in observations and non-instructional roles in the school. During the winter pre-internship, students move to the Professional Development School setting on a full-time basis. During this five-week period, the intern plans and teaches a five to eight day unit and assists the cooperating teacher and the team in a variety of ways. Interns are encouraged to spend time observing in exploratory classes and other classes. After spring break, they return to the same setting for the internship. During the pre-internship and the internship, interns are guided by the on-site college PDS coordinator and the college supervisor to ensure the quality of the experience.

Gordon College

In the Introduction to Early Adolescence and Education course at Gordon College, prospective teachers are assigned to a field site and required to log their thoughts and ideas about the educational process. As the first course of their middle school major, it sets the pattern of continued involvement in middle level schools.

Sophomores plan and implement instruction for small groups in their math methods course. After receiving the topics from the classroom teacher, they assess the children's needs, develop lessons, and teach their topics. Feedback that they receive from the classroom teacher and the college instructor helps them to evaluate themselves as teachers and the children they are instructing. In a reflective portfolio, they record their beliefs about teaching, their strengths and weaknesses, and the beginnings of their philosophy of education.

Junior and seniors take specific middle school courses during which they develop and define the middle school concept and its implementation in schools. In their philosophy and organization class, they plan and design an ideal middle school, developing the rationale for the concept and addressing the unique needs of young adolescents. To prepare for this project, students engage in a shadow study at a local middle school. Prospective teachers follow a middle school student through the academic cycle, gaining perspective on the day from the student's point of view. These perspectives are shared in class and used to write a personal philosophy of education and instruction.

Before the senior student teaching practicum, prospective teachers are placed at their practicum site for the methods and curriculum course. There they engage in inquiry research, surveying and interviewing both students and teachers to gain a better insight into the instructional practices of the school system.

At the end of the course, the seniors meet in seminar and discuss their studies. They reflect on their teacher education program and define their preparation for the profession, their goals, and qualifications to meet the needs of the middle school learners.

5.3   Full time student teaching of at least 10 weeks in grades 5-9, supervised by a qualified teacher and university/college supervisor.

Student teaching has traditionally been seen as the culminating experience of a teacher education program. Student teaching in middle level teacher education should provide prospective teachers with not only a culminating experience of their formal teacher education program, but also an introduction to a full-time teaching career at the middle level.

Georgia College

Prior to the culminating full quarter student teaching experience, students have been introduced to a teaching career at the middle level through an intensive practicum sequence integrated within the block comprised of Language Arts I and II, Reading in the Content Fields courses, and their senior level block sequence of Middle School Curriculum and Instruction. These experiences provide an average of three weeks of full day, in-school time each quarter. In off-campus programs, students are fused into full time practicum experiences throughout their five quarter major sequence, prior to student teaching, with most of the academic course work located in the school site. Inherent in both programs are debriefing seminars conducted as clinical processes to evaluate their experiences. Middle level majors at Georgia College have integrated supervised experiences for at least ten weeks prior to their student teaching. Both programs culminate with a competency-based, ten week student teaching experience supervised and evaluated by the classroom teacher and college supervisor. Because students are already comfortable in classrooms and in directing learning experiences, the student teaching quarter is more productive. The extent of the field-based experiences at Georgia College all but eliminate the apprehension many students experience as they make the transition from student to responsible professional.

West Georgia College

Students in the Middle Grades Education Undergraduate Senior Block Program spend five weeks during the pre-internship (winter quarter) full-time in the schools, and an additional 10 weeks as part of the Internship (spring quarter). During this period of 15 weeks, the intern works in a Professional Development School setting. Cooperating teachers are experienced and recognized as master teachers. As a part of the internship, the school and the department work together to offer several seminars/workshops for interns. While some deal with immediate issues such as classroom management, others deal with job seeking skills, interviewing, professional ethics, and other issues pertinent to entering the teaching field. Some of these are held at the college, involving personnel from outside agencies; others are planned and executed on-site by school administrators and/or faculty. Regularly scheduled planning sessions with college and school faculty members facilitated the cooperative planning required to implement such a program.

Masters

1.1 The curriculum for the masters degree shows depth and breadth in exemplary practice of middle level education. The plan of study for each student builds upon prior professional preparation and experience.

A masters program is designed to provide advanced professional development for teachers. It should provide students with a comprehensive and cohesive program which will enable them to be more effective teachers. A middle level masters program should be more than a set of graduate courses. It should be a well conceived program which has a knowledge base that clearly states the purpose of the program is to provide advanced professional development for middle level educators.

University of Wisconsin-Platteville

The Masters program in Middle Level Education at the University of Wisconsin-Platteville is designed to develop teaching experts who are aware of the developmental stages of their transescent students as well as their own professional developmental needs. The Masters program deepens and broadens the Masters candidates' understanding of the developmental changes experienced by transescents and the implication those changes hold for middle level education and educators, and to build upon prior professional preparation and experience. All middle level courses are block scheduled and team taught.

Middle Level Block I (4 credits) is comprised of Key Concepts of Middle Level Education and Characteristics of Transescents. It is a study of major theories related to the physical, intellectual, emotional, and social (PIES) needs of the transescent. It provides the opportunity to examine the historical foundations as well as the possible future of the middle level movement.

Middle Level Block II (4 credits) is comprised of Advising, Interaction and Communication, and Teaching the Transescent. This block is an examination of appropriate pedagogy for young adolescents, the advisory role of the teacher and appropriate cognitive and affective curricula built upon the developmental needs and concerns of these students.

Middle School Curriculum (3 credits) is the capstone course of the middle level graduate program. It builds on knowledge and understanding of transescents gained in Blocks I and II and provides a forum for the study of issues surrounding middle level curriculum.

Georgia Southern University

Admission to the M.Ed. in Middle Grades Education requires a B.S. Ed. in Middle Grades Education or the completion of the course requirements for certification in middle grades education. The program requires MG 885, Seminar in Middle Grades Education, a course that addresses current issues and research in middle level education. Also, students evaluate the program offered in their school and make recommendations for changes to improve it. In addition, students must take ten hours from three specialized middle school courses that extend their study at the undergraduate level: MG 851, Planning a Middle School Program, MG 852 Interdisciplinary Instruction, and MG 853, Advisor-Advisee and Exploratory Programs: Team Process. All M.Ed. students must take a minimum of ten hours of advanced specialized teaching field courses in two concentrations (to extend their undergraduate preparation) in social studies, math, science, language arts, art, music, and health/physical education. They must also extend their concentrations to a second teaching field. A variety of advanced courses are provided. A field component is included in MG 851, MG 852, MG 853, and MG 855, as well as the advanced subject area courses.

2.1 Major theories and research findings concerning early adolescent development: physical, social, emotional, intellectual, and moral.

Although middle level teachers who are in a masters program should be familiar with the basic needs of young adolescents, it is critical that they develop a clear conceptual theory about how these developmental needs interrelate with one another, as well as how they relate to good middle level practices. It is also critical that these conceptual theories are based on the latest research in the area of young adolescent development.

University of Maine

The Middle Level Education Concentration in the Individually Designed Masters Program (M.Ed.) at the University of Maine uses this standard as both content and as the base of its program. Students in the program have numerous experiences and opportunities to formulate a clear conceptual theory about the interrelationships among the areas of development, as well as how physical, social, emotional, intellectual, and moral development relates to successful practices in middle level schools.

Nearly all M.Ed. students are also practicing middle level teachers, so early in the program through shadow studies, inquiries and careful reading of the historical, research, and contemporary literature, students begin to formulate essential developmental questions, such as: How do the different growth and development areas interrelate, given their discussion in isolation in the literature? What is the influence of various contexts – of school, family, community and peer group – on these developmental issues? How do secondary characteristics of young adolescents as defined by John Hill: autonomy, independence, sexuality, and others, relate to the primary changes of early adolescence?

In the entry level course, EDC 524,Curriculum and Organization of Middle Level Schools, students study these issues as a means of understandomg the variability of development in young adolescents. In EDM 520,Teaching in the Middle Level School, developmental issues are viewed as foundations for the programmatic responses of middle level schools. The importance of advisory programs, for example, lies in their responsiveness to the need for strong adult-student ties, not just because advisory programs are staples in middle level schools. In EML 595, Seminar in Middle Level Education, students pull together their questions and answers from previous courses, as well as through further reading about conceptual theories of early adolescence. In EDG 657, Educational Practicum, a culminating experience of the M.Ed., students have opportunities to "test out" these conceptual theories by working directly with students, teachers and/or parents on an educational practicum.

Across all of these courses, M.Ed. students test their experiential understanding of young adolescents against larger, comprehensive theories of development and apply their understandings into contexts of school, home, family, and peer group. Understanding growth and development at this level is especially important given the low level implementation of developmental knowledge into middle level school practices.

Youngstown State University

Students initially take a human development course in the Psychology Department to clarify the importance of early adolescence in human development (Psych. 906). Students then take a course in education that enables them to apply theories from psychology, sociology, and education to analysis of the relationship between rapid changes in physical, social-emotional, and cognitive development in learners and curriculum/programs (EMCE 938). Students are required to write a major paper synthesizing key concepts about young adolescents and complete a child study in a middle school field-site to broaden their understanding of behaviors in the age-group. Students are expected to distinguish myths from facts about early adolescents and reflect on educational experiences which facilitate cognitive growth, foster self-esteem, and promote social responsibility among early adolescents.

2.2 The history, philosophy, and future development of middle level education.

Students enrolled in middle level masters programs will likely provide much of the leadership for the future development of middle level education. It is thus important that they have a thorough understanding of the history, philosophy and current status of middle level education in order to make informed decisions about the future direction of middle level education.

Appalachian State University

The three specialized middle level education courses required of candidates for the Master of Arts in Middle Grades Education at Appalachian State University are: (a) CI 5170, Teaching the Emerging Adolescent, which focuses on study of the developmental period of young adolescence and the implications of that specialized knowledge for teaching; (b) CI 5190, Middle Level Instruction, which directly addresses successful middle level teaching strategies and related topics; and, (c) CI 5580, Middle Level Curriculum, which includes study of middle school history, the middle school concept and philosophy, the middle level school, and middle level curriculum. Although the key topics included in Guideline 2.2 receive the strongest emphasis in CI 5580, Middle Level Curriculum, they are addressed to some extent in the other two courses. For example, when the developmental period of young adolescence is being studied in CI 5170, Teaching the Emerging Adolescent, the level of accurate knowledge about the age group at the time of various key events, such as the establishment of the junior high school, is discussed. Similarly, the study of teaching strategies commonly used in the junior high and middle schools in the past and present are related to current and future trends and issues in curriculum and instruction.

The primary responsibility for coverage of the content included in Guideline 2.2, however, lies in CI 5580, Middle Level Curriculum. Although middle school curriculum is a major focus of the course, this study is combined with a historical view of the middle level school with emphasis on how this history has influenced curriculum, instruction, and schooling. Background reading for the curriculum component includes *Readings in Middle School Curriculum* (1993) edited by Thomas S. Dickinson and published by NMSA. This book offers an historical perspective on middle school curriculum by including manuscripts written by authorities on middle school curriculum from the 1970s to the 1990s.

Although the Master of Arts Degree in Middle Grades Education was established at Appalachian State University in 1974, it cannot yet be assumed that all graduate students have an understanding of the middle school concept. Many have accepted middle level teaching positions with provisional licensure. Others hold the middle level teaching license they received before specialized middle level preparation became mandatory in 1982. Therefore, the history of the junior high and middle school movements, as well as the components of developmentally responsive middle schools, are emphasized during the first few class periods of CI 5580, Middle Level Curriculum. This knowledge is then drawn upon and enriched as topics such as middle school curriculum and the future development of middle schools are studied. Students are also required to complete a research paper based on their interests and level of specialized knowledge.

The Exemplary Middle School (1993) by Paul S. George and William M. Alexander is also used as a text for CI 5580, Middle Level Curriculum. This excellent resource is useful to both beginning and advanced middle school students. It, in combination with *Readings in Middle School Curriculum* (1993), provides an effective knowledge base both for the class and the total middle school teacher preparation program. These books are supplemented by materials provided by the instructor, especially those focusing on the historical perspectives. Examples of these resources include: (a) The Founders Series from the *Middle School Journal* which spotlights the significant contributions of William M. Alexander, John H. Lounsbury, Gordon F. Vars, Donald H. Eichhorn, and Conrad F. Toepfer; (b) text of the original speech given by William M. Alexander in 1963 at Cornell University when he proposed the new middle school; (c) several chapters from *Perspectives: Middle School Education 1964-1984* (1984) edited by John H. Lounsbury; and, (d) sections from *The Emergent Middle School* (1968) by William M. Alexander and others, and *The Middle School* (1966) by Donald H. Eichhorn.

In summary, topics included in Guideline 2.2, The history, philosophy, and future development of middle level education, receive the most intense study in CI 5580, Middle Level Curriculum. However, the content of this guideline is so much an emphasis of the total program as other middle level courses also focus on the history, philosophy, and future development of middle schools.

University of Kansas

Students study the history, philosophy, and future development of middle level education in C&I 790, Introduction to Middle Level Education. The development of the middle school in the 1990s is placed in historical context with the establishment of junior and senior high schools in the 1920s and the elementary schools in the 19th century. After studying the historical forces influencing school organization, students examine the latest data on the developmental nature of young adolescents. This information is combined with an analysis of changing trends in contemporary society. Given this knowledge base, students are then asked in small groups to design a school that would be appropriate for educating young adolescents for today's world. Students are aided in their investigation by reading *A Middle School Curriculum: From Rhetoric to Reality, 2nd Edition* (Beane, 1993), *Team Organization: Promise – Practices & Possibilities* (Erb & Doda, 1989), *Connecting the Curriculum Through Interdisciplinary Instruction* (Lounsbury, 1992), and *Teaching the Ten to Fourteen Year Old* (Stevenson, 1992). Students are held accountable for their understanding of the philosophical underpinnings of middle school education by writing a defense of such middle school practices as interdisciplinary teaming, teacher advisory, and exploratory curriculum in response to a critic's challenge to these practices.

2.3 Curriculum theory and research focusing on middle level education.

Middle level curriculum is still not well defined in terms of how it differs from being just an extension of elementary curriculum or merely a curriculum designed to specifically prepare students for high school. A masters program in middle level education should provide an educational forum in which the many basic issues surrounding middle level curriculum can be studied based on research and current practice.

Belmont Abbey College

The Masters of Arts in Middle Grades Education program at Belmont Abbey College provides the knowledge and skills that enable teachers to articulate and critically evaluate various theories focusing upon the nature and scope of middle grades curriculum. A review and application of pertinent middle grades research is also a fundamental element. Two courses serve as primary vehicles: ED511, The Middle School: History, Curriculum, and Organization and ED514, Teaching Middle Grades Content: An Analysis of Research and Practice.

ED 511 builds upon the understandings developed in the first graduate course, ED510, The Nature and Needs of Adolescents. An examination of developmental needs and characteristics, including implications for curriculum and instruction, provides a conceptual framework for achieving a broader understanding of the nature of a responsive middle school, including its curriculum. This knowledge, along with the Association for Supervision and Curriculum Development's criteria for a balanced middle grades curriculum, serves as a template for critically examining selected curriculum theories, including classical models that focus upon organized knowledge, personal development, and skills for continued learning, a socio-psychological model (Eichhorn) and other models which tend to focus not only upon skill development and core curriculum, but also upon specific targeted areas such as the arts and health, recreation and physical development. Research regarding various design options for an integrated curriculum is also examined. Students exit with the understanding that middle grades curricula must be responsive and balanced.

ED 514 helps teachers to become more literate consumers of research in middle grades education, including research in curriculum and content teaching fields. Students design research projects pertaining to middle grades education and/or content teaching fields.

California State University - San Bernardino

The California State University, San Bernardino Masters Degree in Education: Middle Grades Option program has been designed thematically to allow graduate students to select a specific theme or strand at the beginning of their graduate studies and progress through the degree program while focusing their efforts and studies on that specific theme.

CSUSB MS. Ed. students select an in-depth study strand/theme from among the following: curriculum and instruction, supervision/administration, adolescent growth and development, school/class environment (culture and climate), or philosophy and foundations. All students in this program are required to complete a culminating project related to their selected strand/theme. Culminating projects may take the form of a qualitative or quantitative thesis or a scholarly project. Implicit in the requirements and design of the thesis or project is the basic belief that such work must demonstrate familiarity and understanding of major theories and research findings concerning early adolescent physical, emotional, social, moral and intellectual development.

Though all program course work includes topics, readings, assignments and action research related to each of the strand/theme areas, students are instructed to focus specifically on the strand/theme they have selected and to prepare their assignments and action research for each class in such a way as to demonstrate their familiarity and understanding of research and theories of early adolescent development. Student selection of their strand/ theme is decided within the first ten quarter units of the program following two introductory overview courses: ESEC 623, Foundations of Middle School Education, and EDUC 663, Introduction to Educational Research. Both of these courses address theories and research related to early adolescent development. ESEC 623, Foundations of Middle School Education traces the development of junior high education and examines social, political, economic, historical, and philosophical bases for junior high education and the eventual development of middle schools. Included in this class is an examination of research related to early adolescent development and the impact of such research upon the development of facilities, programs, instruction, and materials. EDUC 663, Introduction to Educational Research, has been developed to teach graduate students to interpret, analyze, and evaluate research in education with the final objective being the development of a proposal for the students' culminating activity – be it thesis or project.

Finally, the CSUSB Masters Degree in Education - Middle Grades Option Handbook has been developed as a performance based program. Students develop portfolios which are presented as a part of their culminating project. The Handbook contains a series of rubrics developed for each class which require students to demonstrate successful completion and understanding of the knowledge and information presented in each class. Each course rubric includes specific outcomes relating theories and research.

2.4 Pedagogy appropriate for early adolescent learners.

As more research becomes available on the developmental needs of young adolescents and as middle level curriculum becomes more defined, it is important that the pedagogy that links these two become more clearly defined. Courses and experiences within a middle level masters program should enable students to discover the issues involved in making these links.

St. Cloud State University

The chronology, focus, and integrative nature of the core courses in our master's (and endorsement) program(s) enable students to learn about teaching strategies appropriate at the middle level. Early in the program, students are required to take a course on middle school philosophy/organization (ED 624) and one on the developmental characteristics of early adolescents (ED 627). Cooperative and individualistic approaches to teaching are used extensively in each to help students understand developmentally-responsive pedagogy and facilitate these understandings in their professional colleagues, as well as to learn specific course content. The next course in the sequence, Seminar in Early Adolescent Education (ED 625), is an in-depth look at the pedagogical links between early adolescent development and middle level curriculum. Finally, Middle Grades Instructional Strategies (ED 630) and Middle Grades Curriculum (ED 629) are "capstone courses" incorporating techniques for connecting new, abstract content to concrete experiences, teaching formal operational thinking skills, implementing multicultural education, and using authentic assessments in integrative curriculum units or within single-subjects.

Graduate students are also required to complete upper level courses in the various content areas or "teaching fields." Two features of this requirement are consistent with Standard 2.4. First, middle level and teaching field faculty meet periodically to discuss current trends in pedagogy. Secondly, students are encouraged to complete content area courses outside their field of specialization to promote an integrated approach to curriculum/ instruction.

The culminating portfolio, thesis or examination for the master's degree is also consistent with Standard 2.4. Each of these options is driven by the student's unique array of courses and research interests, particularly as they relate to the theory and practice of middle level instruction.

Youngstown State University

The advanced study of pedagogy at Youngstown State University follows courses on the developmental needs of early adolescents and middle grades school organization. The two consecutive quarter series focused on pedagogy begins with an in-depth review of major pedagogical theories (Arnold, 1993; Beane, 1990; Fogarty, 1993; Jacobs, 1989; Lounsbury, 1992; Vars, 1987) and pupil assessment alternatives.

The first course in the series, Appropriate Pedagogy for Early Adolescents (EMCE 990), requires that graduate students identify at least ten curricular organizations designed to increase learning for early adolescents. The students analyze local school curricula to synthesize subject-content principles into significant concepts for interdisciplinary teaching. Students then plan lessons incorporating the selected pedagogical adaptation(s). Students also review pupil assessment literature to identify techniques for systematic observation of pupil performance. The pupil assessment systems frequently selected include pre-and-post tests, attitude surveys and portfolio creation (Perrone, 1991; Schurr, 1992).

During the second course in the series, Action Research in Middle Grade Levels (EMCE 885), students conduct a classroom-based inquiry using the lessons and assessments planned in the preceding course (Stevenson, 1992). The students evaluate pupils' responses to the pedagogical adaptations during and following the teaching. The assessment of pupil response includes evaluation of pupils' problem-solving skills, motivation levels, and knowledge retention. The courses culminate with development of written proposals based on research results for reformation of middle grade level pedagogy and student performance evaluation procedures.

2.5 Advanced study in one or more teaching fields.

Middle level educators have the responsibility of keeping themselves current in their teaching field(s). However, the interdisciplinary nature of middle school curriculum should encourage teachers to expand their knowledge into other fields. A middle level masters program should provide students with the opportunity to take courses that will enhance or expand their content knowledge.

Valdosta State University

Graduate students in the Department of Middle Grades Education at Valdosta State University must enhance and expand their content knowledge in two concentration areas: language arts, social studies, mathematics, or science. They may further their content knowledge base in the same concentration areas as in their basic program, but may select to develop other knowledge bases. For example, if in the basic program, social studies and educational computing were concentration areas, at the masters level, the student might select language arts and social studies to broaden the knowledge base. Usually, because of the advanced content of the academic field courses, students generally take courses in the fields pursued during their bachelor degree.

Course selection in the concentration areas could be a course from social studies such as Methods of Teaching Geography in the Middle School that focuses on land and water forms, relief features, direction and distance, social data, economic information, political information, scientific information, and human factors. Also in the social studies concentration, students could select Children of Minority Cultures that addresses the study of methodology, materials and evaluative strategies for teaching children of minority cultures. If, on the other hand, the concentration area were mathematics, Applications of New Technology in Teaching Middle Grades Mathematics that involves integration of technology into mathematics teaching could be a choice. Another selection in mathematics might be Teaching Problem Solving in Middle School Mathematics with the attention given to development of repertoires of strategies in pupils for solving nonroutine problems and techniques for promoting alternative solutions and methods of attack.

University of Georgia

The master's program at the University of Georgia provides students with the opportunity to take courses that will enhance or expand their content knowledge in one or more teaching fields. Specifically, the master's program at the University of Georgia is a 60 quarter-hour program (i.e., 12 courses); 35 of these quarter hours (i.e., 7 courses) must be taken in content (i.e., language arts, mathematics, science, social science) in at least two areas. These seven courses can be taken in arts and sciences (e.g., The Southern Novel) or in education (e.g., Children's Literature in the Curriculum).

2.6 Culminating examination, project, or thesis that links theory and practice.

Graduate students in a middle level masters program should have the opportunity to reflect about how their program has helped them become a better middle level teacher. To assist them in this process, a middle level masters program should provide some type of culminating activity that provides an opportunity to not only reflect on their courses, but also to project how the experiences they have encountered will help them in the future.

Saginaw Valley State University

The Master's degree program in Middle School Classroom Teaching at Saginaw Valley State University culminates in a three semester credit course (TE 607 - Classroom Teaching: Middle School Seminar) that students are required to take during the last six credits of a thirty-six credit hour program. The course has three components intended to connect theory to practice. These include: 1) a student designed and implemented action research project , 2) two comprehensive take-home examinations, and 3) a discussion of brain-compatible instruction and multiple intelligences as they relate to appropriate practice in the middle grades.

The action research project lasts for six weeks and is implemented in a middle grades classroom or school, usually the student's classroom or school. During the implementation phase of the project, students have individual conferences with the course instructor to review progress and discuss any problems or concerns. The focus of each project is on the teacher as a decision maker. Completed projects are written in thesis format, and bound copies are submitted. The student keeps one copy; one copy is housed in the University's Education Resource Center. Additionally, students present their projects in a forum open to students, faculty, and invited guests.

The take-home examinations ask students to address current issues that affect middle grades practice. Students are expected to take a position on the issue relative to how it affects teacher decision making, and support their position using current literature as well as their experience. Students are encouraged to draw on knowledge gained from previous course work and their action research project in the responses. Each examination is read and scored by at least three faculty. To control for bias, exams are read blind, i.e., faculty are unaware of who has written the exam.

The discussion of brain-compatible instruction and multiple intelligences stems from the textbooks for the course. Students are assigned a chapter in a text, the main points of the chapter are outlined by the students, and students lead seminar participants in a discussion of the implications for middle grades teaching.

University of Northern Colorado

The University of Northern Colorado Middle School Masters Program strives to make its program an integrated whole rather than just a set of unrelated courses that lead toward a degree. The Middle School Practicum was developed to help students see the interrelationship among the concepts presented in the various courses in the students' program. The Practicum is also intended to help the students see the practical application of these concepts to the middle school setting.

During the latter part of the students' program, they will identify a project which would: (1) apply what they have learned in their program to their own teaching and (2) enhance their school. After they have submitted a proposal to their graduate advisor for approval, they will carry out the project and write a formal report. The report is comprehensive and contains the following sections: introduction, rationale, review of related literature, description of the project, and a discussion of the impact of the project on the student's teaching and/or school.

Although the Middle School Practicum has proven valuable for helping students gain a more comprehensive view of middle level education, the faculty of UNC wanted further assurance that students were reflecting on what they were learning throughout the program. In 1991 a pilot project was begun which gave a select group of students the opportunity to develop portfolios as they went through the program rather than take written comprehensives at the end of their program. Those students completed their program in the spring of 1994. The use of portfolios proved to be an extremely valuable tool for helping students engage in an ongoing reflection process throughout their program.

Initial Licensure Beyond the Bachelor's

Although the NMSA/NCATE guidelines address four distinct levels of middle level teacher preparation, there are a growing number of colleges and universities which, by design, have developed programs which overlap one or more of these sets of guidelines. This is particularly true of programs which overlap the basic and masters guidelines. Rather than ignore the existence of such programs, the authors have chosen to include this section which will attempt to explain the importance of such programs in the preparation of middle level teachers. Most of these programs meet the guidelines of both the respective overlapping levels. However, some may only meet one but not the other, or partially meet both but not fully meet either.

These programs can usually be classified into the following three categories: five year/fifth year programs, Master of Arts in Teaching (Education), and post baccalaureate programs. Although these three categories represent distinctly different approaches to preparing middle level teachers, they also have the following characteristics in common:

1. Students may take course work at either the undergraduate or the graduate levels.

2. Students who enroll in such programs have generally completed a bachelors degree in liberal arts or a field unrelated to teaching, or they have completed a bachelors degree as a part of an extended program.

3. Credit earned in these programs will lead toward initial licensing or toward an additional teaching certification.

4. The majority of the course work required in these programs is pedagogical in nature rather than subject matter oriented, except in extended programs which involve both.

5. Graduate work taken in these programs will generally apply to a masters degree in education while at the same time count toward an initial license for teaching at the middle level.

There are several reasons for the increased demand for these programs. One of the most common reasons is that many colleges and universities have found it necessary to extend their programs from four years to five years, particularly in states where teachers are required to have a liberal arts degree as a part of their teacher preparation program. It has become very difficult, if not impossible, for students to meet the requirements within four years for a liberal arts degree and also complete all the courses and field experiences necessary to adequately prepare them for teaching.

Although these programs are often referred to as fifth year teacher education programs, there is a distinct difference between a fifth year program and a five year program. Many of the Holmes Group Universities have subscribed to a fifth year program as have some states such as California. In a typical fifth year program teacher education candidates would concentrate on obtaining a liberal arts degree during their first four years of college and then take their teacher education courses during the fifth year. A five year teacher education program, on the other hand, allows the students to take their education courses throughout their five year program.

A second reason for the growing popularity of these programs is the increasing number of individuals who are choosing teaching as a second career. As the job market becomes more and more unstable, particularly at the white collar levels, more and more people are seeking teaching as an alternative career choice. Also, as our society becomes more mobile, people are asked to relocate. This often requires their spouses to change their careers; many of whom take the opportunity to enter the teaching profession.

Another reason these programs are in demand is the growing number of middle school teachers who are currently teaching under an elementary or secondary teaching license and now wish to add a middle level license endorsement. An overwhelming number of teachers in our middle level schools are either licensed at the secondary or elementary levels. Very few have an official license to teach at the middle level. The reason is very apparent. When most of these teachers went through their initial preparation programs, there were only a few colleges and universities that offered any type of middle level preparation programs. In addition, there were no incentives to have such programs because very few states had adopted any certification standards for the middle school level. This situation has improved over the last few years, but there are still only three states of the 33 states which claim to have some type of middle level license or endorsement that require teachers to have a middle level license in order to teach at this level. The remaining states have overlapping certification which allows both elementary and secondary licensed teachers to teach at the middle level.

Listed below are selected colleges and universities which have developed programs that not only offer graduate credit, thus addressing the NMSA/NCATE masters guidelines, but also within those same programs offer initial middle level certification, thus addressing the NMSA/NCATE basic guidelines.

> University of Kansas
> Ohio University
> North Carolina State University
> University of Northern Colorado
> University of Toledo
> Williamette University
> University of Wisconsin - Eau Claire

The University of Kansas middle level program is a five year program in which the students complete a baccalaureate degree and then take a fifth year to complete their middle school certification program. Although many of the middle level courses and field experiences are taken during this fifth year, students can begin taking courses and become involved in field experiences as early as their freshman year. Most of the courses taken during the student's fifth year can be taken for graduate credit and applied toward a masters degree in curriculum and instruction. The five year program allows students to pursue a single certification at the middle level or a dual certification at middle level and elementary or middle level and secondary.

"The Ohio University graduate program in middle school education leading to certification recognizes and reflects both national and state trends that provide alternative routes to teacher certification. The program permits the student to receive a master's degree and complete teacher certification requirements at the graduate level. It recognizes that post-baccalaureate students often have background experience relevant to the classroom and therefore can profit from graduate study leading to certification rather than enrolling in an undergraduate certification program." This is a direct quote from the stated purpose of the Ohio University Master of Education Emphasis Middle School Education Program. Students must also have content preparation in two fields. These courses my be taken either at the undergraduate or graduate levels. Other approved graduate courses may be included in the students' masters program.

The University of Wisconsin - Eau Claire has had a Masters of Education - Professional Development Program since 1983. Students are not only able to obtain their masters in education, but also further their professional development by strengthening and extending their certification. Middle level certification in Wisconsin has not been in great demand because of the overlapping among the different certification levels. The University of Wisconsin - Eau Claire program gives students an opportunity to take courses that would directly apply to middle level certification. Although obtaining a masters and receiving certification are not mutually exclusive, they do have a great deal of overlap. One of the things that makes the University of Wisconsin - Eau Claire program unique is its ability to take the program off campus and tailor-make it to fit the needs of a particular educational community. More than half of the courses in the program directly relate to middle level education, leaving some flexibility in how the remaining courses could be adapted to meet the individual needs of a student, particular school or school district. The School of Education at UW-Eau Claire is currently working toward a 5-9 certification program that will be correlated with a baccalaureate degree.

The North Carolina State Middle Grades Education "A+G" Program is designed for adults with non-education baccalaureate degrees who wish to become teachers of grades 6-9. Students receive their certification in middle grades in the areas of social studies or language arts. They are required to take a minimum of 45 semester hours which include course work in either language arts or social studies. The remaining hours are comprised of graduate and/or undergraduate education courses. In addition, students experience a 10-week teaching internship.

The Post Baccalaureate Non Degree Licensure Program at the University of Northern Colorado basically attracts two types of students: students who have a bachelors degree and wish to enter the field of middle level teaching and students who are already teaching in middle level schools under another license and would like to add the middle level license to their existing license. Courses may be taken at the graduate or undergraduate levels depending on the student's background. All students must take the middle level core block of courses. Those students who do not hold a current teaching license must take the professional teacher education block of courses, which includes student teaching. In addition, all student must show that they have content preparation in at least two fields.

The University of Toledo's Middle Grades Certification Program provides Ohio teachers currently holding elementary or secondary certificates with the opportunity to gain teaching certification in grades 4 to 9. The program is unique in that it is basically a graduate level program for teachers presently possessing elementary or secondary certificates. Teachers may choose to apply the graduate credit they receive in this program toward a masters degree in curriculum. The program requires that students have content preparation in two of the following fields: language arts, mathematics, social studies, or science. Although the students in this program are experienced teachers, they must still take at least two credit hours of supervised field experience as a part of their 18-24 credit hours of course work in pedagogy.

Although there is no middle level certification in Oregon, Willamette University has taken the initiative in developing a middle level teacher preparation program. Instead of receiving a middle level certification from the state, graduates receive a special certificate through the university verifying they have completed a Willamette University sanctioned program for specialized preparation in middle level education. Student must earn an Oregon Basic Teaching License with an elementary endorsement or an elementary with at least one secondary subject area endorsement. The program is designed to reflect middle level philosophy and practice. Middle level courses are team taught. Courses are taught in interrelated blocks. A variety of traditional and alternative assessment techniques are used to evaluate students. Students are given hands-on experiences by spending over a 1000 clock hours in middle schools. In addition, students are assigned to a cohort group for advisement and support throughout their program.

Specialist

The specialist degree programs from responding institutions are designed to provide the student with additional academic depth and enrichment in a field of study without the major research focus present in most doctoral programs. The following institutions shared information on specialist degree programs in middle level education:

> University of Georgia
> Georgia Southern University
> Valdosta State University
> Western Carolina University

The program at the University of Georgia requires 50 quarter hours beyond the master's degree and contains course work in four areas: young adolescent development, middle school education, teaching field specialization, and research. Graduates study at least two teaching fields, complete an applied research project, and must pass a final comprehensive examination.

The specialist program at Georgia Southern University is a 45 quarter hour program beyond the master which allows students to complete 25 quarter hours of course work in two areas of concentration, a series of advanced courses focusing on the developmental needs of middle level learners, and fifteen credit hours of course work in a research sequence. The sequence includes a seminar and field study in middle level education and leads to the completion of a major research paper.

Valdosta State College offers a sixth year program leading to a specialist degree that requires 105 quarter hours beyond the bachelors degree. Students have considerable flexibility in selecting course work in adolescent psychology, foundations, and research trends in middle level education. The thesis requirement may be a written research paper or a field project relating to the students' work in their own school.

The specialist program at Western Carolina University gives master teachers at the middle level who wish to continue in their professional growth an appropriate option for future study. Course work includes 36 semester hours in the following areas: advanced study in a field of concentration, specific course work in middle level education, and a research project to be carried out in classrooms. In addition, students will develop a professional portfolio throughout the program. They will make a presentation of their portfolio to selected teachers, administrators, central offices personnel, and university faculty as the capstone experience for the Ed. S. degree.

Doctoral

At the time of this writing, the University of Georgia was the only university with a free standing doctoral degree programs in middle level education. Four other higher education institutions which did not have a free standing doctoral program in middle level education, but offered opportunities for students to take substantial middle level course work at the doctoral level submitted their program for consideration for this publication. These are briefly described.

University of Georgia

Ph.D. candidates in the University of Georgia's Middle School Doctoral program have the opportunity to develop their own individualized program under the guidance a graduate faculty advisor. The student's program may includes course work from a variety of departments. Students are encouraged to develop strands of related research that bring together disciplines or content areas.

The program has a strong research component which emphasizes both quantitative and qualitative research and fosters methodologies which combine these two approaches. The program contains course work which stress the following area: young adolescents and schools, history of reform in the education of young adolescents, comparative and international perspective on the education of young adolescents, multicultural education and sociocultural issues in early adolescence, and middle school curriculum.

Doctoral Programs with Emphasis of Middle Level

With the exception of the University of Georgia, most middle level doctoral programs are nested within existing doctoral program such as Educational Leadership, Curriculum and Instruction, or Elementary Education.

University Of Nebraska. A student enrolling in the program at the University of Nebraska can take an area of concentration of up to 20 semester credit hours in the area of middle level education in addition to the dissertation. The two supporting areas of Educational Administration and Curriculum and Instruction are strongly recommended to support field work and program development. Middle level is identified as an area of concentration with the degree major of Administration, Curriculum, and Instruction.

University of Arizona. The University of Arizona doctorate in Curriculum and Instruction allows for 12 hours of specific course work in middle level curriculum, up to six hours of internship, a minor of up to 15 hours in a related field and dissertation research. The program allows students to obtain a specialization in middle level while also considering broad educational issues in curriculum theory and development.

University of Northern Iowa. Students attending the University of Northern Iowa can select an intensive study area in Curriculum and Instruction with Middle Level Education as a related field. The program allows a student to select up to 15 semester hours of course work specifically in middle level education along with practicum and dissertation research.

University of Northern Colorado. The doctoral program in Elementary Education at the University of Northern Colorado allows a student to select from 12-18 hours of specific course work in middle level education along with dissertation research. In addition, students may develop a cognate area of specialization relating to their subject area interest. The focus of the program is to cultivate student expertise in program development, pedagogy appropriate for higher education, and curriculum leadership.■

4. The Key to the Future of Middle Level Education

When one reflects back on progress made in middle level certification/licensure over the past twenty years, there is much to celebrate. The National Middle School Association provided a sorely needed forum to coordinate efforts to reform middle level teacher education. Defined standards and guidelines have been established. These have emerged from the conceptual base for middle level education, have been developed within NCATE, and have been field tested through the folio review process. Through consistent leadership, with a focused and well-defined mission, NMSA has provided individuals, institutions, and agencies with information and personal assistance which emphasize the need for preparing teachers for the middle level.

Examination of the mission statements of institutions of higher education offering teacher education programs and those of state departments of education, with few exceptions, indicates acceptance of a responsibility to provide leadership in reform and a commitment to meet present and future needs of educators. Even though the preparation of middle level teachers has been included as a part of many of these reform efforts, a strong commitment to include specialized preparation of middle level teachers as a high priority at university and state department levels is still lacking.

There are many challenges yet to be faced before the preparation of teachers of young adolescents has achieved the same status as the preparation of elementary or secondary teachers. Listed below are a few of the major challenges we must aggressively address if appropriate preparation of teachers for young adolescents is to become a reality.

- State must provide initial licensing for middle school teachers that minimize any overlap with elementary and secondary.

- States must require beginning teachers to have a middle level license to teach in designated middle level grades.

- Certification standards must be developed which allow middle level teachers who currently do not have a middle level license to obtain a middle level certification. This type of certification should take into consideration their previous teaching experience as well as be an integral part of their professional development plan.

- Correlation and coordination of the NMSA/NCATE guidelines with state middle level licensure/certification standards must be extended.

- Further development and implementation of teacher education programs that directly reflect the NMSA/NCATE guidelines is needed.

- A coordinated effort between NMSA, state departments of education, and higher education institutions must be developed and implemented to assess and sustain the quality of middle level teacher education programs.

- More middle school teacher education programs must be developed which utilize the expertise of practitioners in the field through such programs as professional development schools.

Recent data indicate that of 715 AACTE member institutions, 243 have program elements specifically directed at the preparation of middle level teachers (NMSA, 1992). Although 243 programs may seem like a substantial number of programs, one must keep in mind that only a minority of these programs actually are stand alone programs. Most are add-on programs to an elementary or secondary program or may represent only one or two courses on middle level education (NMSA, 1992). In addition the bulk of the middle school programs in these 243 schools have small enrollments, and thus the number of actual middle level teachers effected by these programs is minuscule in comparison to the number of middle school teachers needed in the field. This monograph, along with the other literature reviewed in this publication, identifies a number of comprehensive programs that reflect the diversity of approaches used to accomplish a common standard. Progress continues to be made both at the basic level as well as the advanced levels in middle level teacher education.

There are many encouraging signs. The majority of states now have some licensure/certification for those seeking a separate endorsement for middle level teaching. Since introducing the NMSA/NCATE guidelines in 1990, two-thirds of the programs submitted to the NCATE Folio Review Process met the NMSA guidelines (Swaim, 1993). The results of folio reviews indicate there are many approaches used to meet the guidelines. Problems still exist with components often imbedded within elementary or secondary preparation programs in which efforts to address the unique needs of middle level learners are dependent upon decisions made by a specific professor.

Now is the time to establish consistency among the states and across programs of teacher preparation for middle level students. This is not meant to control how teachers are being prepared, but to insure that future teachers are exposed to what middle level teachers should know and be expected to do, and that they have demonstrated that they can do these things as professional practitioners. Efforts at the national level, including initiatives by

NMSA, NCATE, and the National Board for Professional Teaching Standards, are providing an increased awareness of the importance of having professionals who are knowledgeable about what young adolescents need and who can also contribute to creating an educational environments that is developmentally appropriate.■

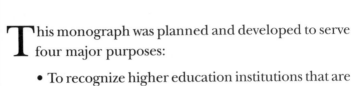

Epilogue

This monograph was planned and developed to serve four major purposes:

• To recognize higher education institutions that are currently taking a lead in the preparation of middle level teachers.

• To provide examples of how middle school teacher education programs can meet the National Middle School Association/National Council for Accreditation of Teacher Education guidelines.

• To encourage other institutions to develop middle level teacher education programs.

• To develop a network among middle level teacher education programs that would promote the preparation of middle level teachers.

By citing characteristics of thirty-eight higher education institutions that have middle level teacher education programs, and showing how these programs meet NMSA/NCATE guidelines, the authors feel confident that they have successfully met the first two purposes of the study. Time will tell if the last two purposes will be met. Even if a formal network is never realized between those having programs, an informal network has been formed by the mere fact that institutions wishing to develop a middle level teacher education program now have a list of resources to which they can turn.

The original NMSA/NCATE guidelines provide the benchmarks for middle level teacher education. But even benchmarks need constant review and assessment to assure they represent the best practices. Over the last six years the guidelines have undergone continual review and assessment. This feedback is carefully considered and procedural changes are made where necessary. However, changes to the guidelines themselves are made only every fifth year.

The original guidelines underwent an official revision process in 1995. The revised guidelines were approved by the NMSA Board of Trustees and by NCATE in the summer and fall of 1995 respectively. When NMSA submitted the revised guidelines to NCATE, they were required to declare whether major revisions were made which would require already approved middle level teacher education programs to submit new folios. It was the position of NMSA that the revisions were not major and previously approved programs should not be required to submit new folios.

The original NMSA/NCATE guidelines are set forth in Appendix A, while the revised NMSA/NCATE guidelines are in Appendix B. Charts showing the relationship of the revised guidelines to the original guidelines comprise Appendix C. Although the format of the revised guidelines look significantly different, it is evident by looking at the chart that most of the revisions were either expansions, clarifications, or consolidations of the original guidelines. Of the 28 revised basic guidelines only three were new, while two of the original basic guidelines were eliminated. There were more new guidelines at the advanced level, but still most of the guidelines were either expansions, clarifications, or consolidations of the original guidelines.

The authors are pleased to include the new revised NMSA/NCATE guidelines as a part of this monograph. As new middle level teacher education programs are developed using the revised guidelines perhaps another monograph entitled *Raising the Standards: Improving Middle Level Teacher Education* will be developed. ■

Resource List of Contributing
Higher Education Institutions

The higher education institutions listed below should be recognized for being on the forefront of middle level teacher education. It is because of the efforts of dedicated faculty members who work within those institutions that teachers are now being prepared to work with young adolescents in our middle schools across the nation. Without these pioneer programs, middle level teacher education would not have the knowledge and experience to draw upon in order to further the preparation of middle level teachers in the future.

One of the purposes for this project was to help build a network among higher education institutions that are interested in middle level teacher education. You are encouraged to contact any of these schools if you are interested in further information about their programs. Contributing faculty members at the time this publication was written are listed.

Schools	Guidelines	Pages
C. Kenneth McEwin Dept. of Curriculum and Instruction Appalachian State University Boone, NC 28608	M (2.2)	p. 81
David Kommer 323 Bixler Hall Ashland University Ashland, OH 44907	B(3.10,3.11)	pp. 61, 62

Jackie Ennis Dept. of Education Barton College Wilson, OR 27893	B(3.7)	p. 56
Larry Allred Dept. of Education Belmont Abbey College Belmont, NC 28012	M(2.3)	p. 85
Leo Anglin 5019 Berry College Mount Berry, GA 30149	B (4.3)	p. 70
Irvin Howard 5500 University Parkway California St. Univ., San Bernardino San Bernardino, CA 92827	M(2.3)	p. 86
Peggy Gaskill Department. of Teacher Ed. and Professional Development Central Michigan University Mt. Pleasant, MI 48859	B(2.2, 3.5)	pp. 38, 51
Donald Bragaw East Carolina University Greenville, NC 27858-4353	B(3.2, 3.4)	pp. 46, 49
Charles Carter Box 860 Elizabeth City State College Elizabeth City, NC 27909	B(3.1, 3.3)	pp. 44, 48
Rebecca Lovett Middle Grades Education Georgia College Milledgeville, GA 31061	B(5.1, 5.3)	pp. 72, 75

Michael Allen	B(3.7)	p. 56
Georgia Southern University	M(1.1)	p. 78
LB 8134	Specialist	p. 100
Statesboro. GA 30460		
Janis Flint Ferguson	B(5.2)	p. 74
255 Grapevine Road		
Gordan College		
Wenham, MA 01984		
Deborah Curtis		
and Savario Mungo	B(2.3, 3.5,3.9)	pp. 41, 52,
Box 5330		58
Illinios State University		
Normal, IL 61790-5330		
Thomas Erb	M(2.2)	p. 84
Bailey Hall 202	Lic. beyond Bach	pp. 94-100
Univ. of Kansas		
Lawrence, KS 66045-2340		
John Arnold	B(4.3)	p. 70
Department. of C&I	Lic. beyond Bach.	pp. 94-100
North Carolina State University		
Raleigh, NC 27695-7801		
Judy Long	B(3.6,3.8)	pp. 54, 57
Education Dept.		
North Georgia College		
Dahlonega, GA 30597		
Monroe Johnson	Lic. beyond Bach.	pp. 94-100
College of Education		
Ohio University		
Athens, OH 45701		
Ervin Sparapani	M(2.6)	p. 92
7400 Bay Road		
Saginaw Valley State University		
University Center, MI 40710		

David Hough 901 South National Avenue Southwest Missouri State University Springfield, MO 65804	B(3.6, 3.12)	pp. 55, 64
Walter Ullrich & Terry Miller 720 4th Avenue S. St. Cloud State University St. Cloud, MN 56301	B(3.3) M(2.4)	p. 49 p. 88
Donald Clark Department of Teaching and Teacher Education. University of Arizona Tucson, AZ 85721	Doctoral	p. 103
Denise Muth Glynn Dept. of Elementary Education Univ. of Georgia Athens, GA 30602	B(1.1, 2.2) M(2.5) Specialist Doctoral	pp. 34, 40 p. 91 p. 100 p. 102
Edward Brazee 5766 Shibles Hall University of Maine Orono, ME 04469	M(2.1)	p. 79
Alfred Arth Henzel Hall 215 University of Nebraska Lincoln, NE 68588-0355	Doctoral	p. 103
David Strahan and John Van Hoose School of Education UNC Greensboro Greensboro, NC 27412-5001	B(2.1, 4.1, 5.1)	pp. 36, 65, 72
Barbara Whinery McKee Hall 213 University of N. Colorado Greeley, CO 80639	B(3.10, 3.11,) M(2.6) Lic. beyond Bach. Doctoral	pp. 60, 62 p. 93 pp. 94-11 p. 103

Donna Schumacher
and Greg Stefanich   B(3.4, 3.9, 4.1)   pp. 50, 59, 66
618 Schindler Ed. Ctr.   Doctoral   p. 103
University of Northern Iowa
Cedar Falls, IA 50614-0606

Dwayne DeMedio   Lic. beyond Bach.   pp. 94-100
2801 West Bancroft St.
University of Toledo
Toledo, OH 43606

Ann Lockledge   B(3.1, 4.2)   pp. 45, 68
Dept. of Curriculum Studies
UNC Wilmington
Wilmington, NC 28403

Jerry Rottier & Margie Stone   Lic. beyond Bach.   pp. 94-100
C&I Dept.
UW Eau Claire
Eau Claire, WI 54702-4004

Tom Lo Guidice & Alison Bunte M(1.1)   p. 77
School of Education
University of Wisconsin, Platteville
Platteville, WI 53818

Martin Tadlock   B(2.3)   p. 42
Dept. of Elementary Education
Utah State University
Logan, Utah 84322-2805

Adele Ducharme   B(3.12, 4.2)   pp. 64, 68
Department of Middle   M(2.5)   p. 90
Grades Education   Specialist   p. 100
Valdosta State University
Valdosta, GA 31698

Deborah Stiles & Kay Easton   B(2.1)   p. 37
470 East Lockwood
Webster University
St. Louis, MO 63119

John Myers   B(5.2, 5.3)   pp. 73, 76
School of Education
West Georgia College
Carrollton, GA 30118

Victoria Faircloth   Specialist   p. 100
Department. of Elementary
Education. & Reading
Western Carolina University
Cullawhee, NC 28723

Nancy Minix   B(1.1, 3.2)   pp. 35, 47
Dept. of Teacher Education
Western Kentucky University
Bowling Green, KY 42101

Rosalyn Edelson   Lic. beyond Bach.   pp. 94-100
Education Dept.
Willamette University
Salem, OR 97301

Nancie Shillington   M(2.1, 2.4)   p. 80, 89
410 Wick Avenue
Youngstown State University
Youngstown, OH 44555

References

Alexander, W. M., & McEwin, C. K. (1982). *The status of middle/junior high school teacher education programs: A research report.* Boone, NC: Appalachian State University.

Alexander, W. M., Williams, E. L., Compton, M., Hines, V. A., & Prescott, D. (1968). *The emergent middle school.* New York: Holt, Rinehart, & Winston.

Alexander, W. M., & McEwin, C. K. (1989). *Schools in the middle: Status and progress.* Columbus, OH: National Middle School Association.

Alexander, W. M., & McEwin, C. K. (1988). *Preparing to teach at the middle level.* Columbus, OH: National Middle School Association.

Beane, J. A., & Lipka, R. P. (1987). *When the kids come first: Enhancing self esteem.* Columbus, OH: National Middle School Association.

Beane, J. A. (1993). *A middle school curriculum: From rhetoric to reality* (2nd ed). Columbus, OH: National Middle School Association.

Brazee, E. N., & Capelluti, J. (1995). *Dissolving boundaries: Toward an integrative curriculum.* Columbus, OH: National Middle School Association.

Burnkrant, S. J. (1991). *Where will our program take us? A compilation of state middle school certification requirements.* National Collegiate Middle School Association.

Butler, D. A., & Dickinson, T. S. (1991). *On site: Preparing middle level teachers through field experience.* Columbus, OH: National Middle School Association.

Carnegie Council on Adolescent Development (1989). *Turning points:Preparing American youth for the 21st century.* New York: Carnegie Corporation of New York.

Cawelti, G. (1988). Middle schools a better match with early adolescent needs, ASCD survey finds. *ASCD Curriculum Update* Alexandria, VA: Association for Curriculum Development.

Cole, C. G. (1988). *Guidance in the middle school: Everyone's responsibility.* Columbus, OH: National Middle School Association.

Compton ,M. F. & Hawn, H. C. (1993). *Exploration: The total curriculum.* Columbus, OH: National Middle School Association.

DeMedio, D., & Stewart, M. (1990). *Attitudes toward middle grade certification: A national survey.* NASSP Bulletin, 64-71.

Douglass, A. A. (1920). *The junior high school.* Bloomington, IN: National Study of Education.

Doda, N. M. (1981). *Teacher to teacher.* Columbus, OH: National Middle School Association.

Erb, T. O., & Doda, N. M. (1989). *Team organization: Promise, practice and possibilities.* Washington, D C. National Education Association.

Erb, T. O. (Ed.). (1995). Reforming middle grade teacher Preparation. *Middle School Journal, 26* (5).

Eichhorn, D. H. (1966). *The middle school.* New York: The Center for Applied Research in Education, Inc.

Epstein, J. L., & Mac Iver, D. J. (1990). *Education in the middle grades: National practice and trends.* Columbus, OH: National Middle School Association.

George, P. S., & Shewey, K. (1994). *New evidence for the middle school.* Columbus, OH: National Middle School Association.

Goodlad, J. I. (1990). *Teachers for our nation's schools.* San Francisco, CA: Jossey-Bass.

Gillan, R. E. (1978). *A national assessment of the effects of middle school teacher certification.* Unpublished doctoral dissertation. Evanston, IL: Northwestern University.

Hoversten, C., Doda, N. M., & Lounsbury, J. H. (1991). *Treasure chest: A teacher advisory source book.* Columbus, OH: National Middle School Association.

Irvin, J. L. (1992). *Transforming middle level education: Perspectives and possibilities.* Needham Heights, MA: Allyn & Bacon.

James, M. (1986). *Advisor-advisee programs: Why, what and how.* Columbus, OH: National Middle School Association.

Lounsbury, J. H. (1992). *Connecting the curriculum through interdisciplinary instruction.* Columbus, OH: National Middle School Association.

McEwin, C. K., & Allen, M.G. (1983). *Middle level teacher certification: A National study.* Boone, NC: Appalachian State University.

McEwin, C. K. (1992). *Middle level teacher education directory.* Columbus, OH: National Middle School Association.

McEwin, C. K., & Dickinson, T. S. (1995). *The professional preparation of middle level teachers: Profiles of successful programs.* Columbus, OH: National Middle School Association.

McEwin, C. K., Dickinson T. S., & Erb, T. O., Scales, P. C. (1995). *A vision of excellence: Organizing principles for middle grades teacher preparation.* Carrboro, NC: Center for Early Adolescence, University of North Carolina at Chapel Hill & Columbus, OH: National Middle School Association.

Merenbloom, E. Y. (1991). *The team process in the middle school: A handbook for teachers.* Columbus, OH: National Middle School Association.

Miller, J. M., & Darling-Hammond, L. (1994). *Model standards for beginning teacher licensing and development: A resource for state Dialogue.* Unpublished paper developed by the Interstate New Teacher Assessment and Support Consortium, Washington, D. C.: Council of Chief State School Officers.

National Association of State Directors of Teacher Education and Certification (1993). *NASDTEC outcome-base standards and portfolio assessment: Outcome-base teacher education standards for the elementary, middle and high school levels, 2nd ed.* Seattle, WA: Author.

National Board for Professional Teaching Standards (1992). *Early adolescence/English language arts standards for board certification.* Washington, D. C.: Author.

National Board for Professional Teaching Standards (1992). *Early ado-lescence/generalist standards for board certification.* Washington, D. C.: Author.

National Middle School Association (1991). *Professional certification and preparation for the middle level: A position paper of the National Middle School Association.* Columbus, OH: Author.

National Middle School Association (1991). *National Middle School Association curriculum guideline handbook.* Columbus, OH: Author.

National Middle School Association (1992). *This we believe.* Columbus, OH: Author.

National Middle School Association (1995). *This we believe: Developmentally responsive middle level schools.* Columbus, OH: Author.

Pumerantz, P. (1969). Few state certify teachers for growing middle schools. *Phi Delta Kappa, 51* (102).

Scales, P. C. (1991). A portrait of young adolescents in the 1990's: *Implications for promoting healthy growth and development.* Carrboro, NC: Center for Early Adolescence's, University of North Carolina at Chapel Hill.

Scales, P. C. (1992). *Windows of opportunity: Improving middle grades teacher preparation.* Carrboro, NC: Center for Early Adolescence, University of North Carolina at Chapel Hill.

Scales, P. C., & McEwin, C. K. (1994). *Growing Pains: The making of America's middle school teachers.* Columbus, OH: National Middle School Association.

Swaim, J. H. (1991). Reform of teacher education: The implications for middle level. *Middle School Journal, 22* (4), 47-51.

Swaim, J. H. (1993). National Middle School Association supports Carnegie recommendations. *NCATE Quality Teaching, 2*(2), 10.

Stefanich, G., Wills, F., Buss, R. (in press). The use of interdisciplinary teaming and its influence on student self-concept in middle school. *Journal of Early Adolescent Research.*

Stevenson, C. (1992). *Teaching 10-14 year olds.* New York: Longman Publishing Group.

Toepfer, C. F. (1986). Stress and suicides in middle level schools: *Middle School Journal.* Columbus, OH: National Middle School Association.

Valentine, J. W., & Morgar, D. C. (1992). Middle level certification - An encouraging evolution. *Middle School Journal, 24*(2), 36-43.

Van Hoose, J., & Strahan, D. B. (1988). *Young adolescent development and school practices: Promoting harmony.* Columbus, OH: National Middle School Association.

VanTil, W., Vars, G. F., & Lounsbury, J. H. (1961). *Modern education for the junior high school years.* New York: Bobbs-Merrill Company.

APPENDIX A

Original NMSA/NCATE-Approved Teacher Education Curriculum Guidelines

BASIC

1. **Basic Program**
   1.1 An identifiable program is established for prospective middle level teachers.

2. **Nature and Needs of Early Adolescents**
   2.1 Understanding the physical, social, emotional, intellectual, and moral development of early adolescents in various social contexts.
   2.2 Plan the teaching/learning process to facilitate early adolescent development.
   2.3 Create and maintain a developmentally responsive program and learning environment.

3. **Middle School Philosophy, Curriculum, and Instruction**
   3.1 Articulate and apply a sound philosophy of middle level education.
   3.2 Apply an understanding of the organizational structures appropriate for middle level learners (such as: interdisciplinary teaming, block-time, cross graded groupings.
   3.3 Understand and implement a balanced and integrated middle level curriculum which includes:
   3.3.1 Skills for continued learning.
   3.3.2 Organized knowledge.

3.3.3 Exploratory and enrichment opportunities

3.3.4 Teacher based guidance.

3.4 Understanding the interrelationships among the fields of knowledge.

3.5 Adapt curriculum and instruction to the learning patterns of each student.

3.6 Facilitate student's personal growth through: appropriate personal relationships.

3.7 Foster active learning by employing a variety of classroom grouping patterns including small group work and independent study.

3.8 Teach problem solving and communication skills (reading, listening, writing, and speaking) as an integral part of all instruction.

3.9 Perform guidance roles in formal and informal settings.

3.10 Provide leadership for student activities.

3.11 Employ evaluation procedures appropriate for early adolescents.

3.12 Work collaboratively with teachers, staff members, parents, resource persons, and community groups.

4. **Teaching Field and Methodology**

4.1 Teaching fields are broad. interdisciplinary and encompass the major areas within those fields. At least one field is required but preparation in two different areas is preferred.

4.2 When preparation in two fields is provided, those fields should be different (science and mathematics, not biology and chemistry)

4.3 At least one methods course designed specifically for teaching at the middle level should be provided.

5. Field Experience

    5.1 Early and continuing field involvement in grades 5-9.

    5.2 Observation, participation, and teaching experiences ranging from individual to large group settings.

    5.3 Full-time student teaching of at least 10 weeks in grades 5-9, supervised by a qualified teacher and a university/college supervisor.

MASTERS

1. The curriculum for the masters degree shows depth and breadth in the study of the theoretical base and exemplary practice of middle level education. The plan of study for each student builds upon prior professional preparation and experience.

2. Programs leading to the masters degree in middle level education include the following:

    2.1 Major theories and research findings concerning early adolescent development: physical,, social, emotional, intellectual, and moral.

    2.2 The history, philosophy, and future development of middle school education.

    2.3 Curriculum theories and research focusing on middle level education.

    2.4 Pedagogy appropriate for early adolescent learners.

    2.5 Advanced study in one or more teaching fields.

    2.6 A culminating examination, project, or thesis that links theory and practice.

SPECIALIST

1. The curriculum for the specialists degree shows depth an breath in the study of the theoretical base and exemplary practice of middle level education. The plan of study for each student builds upon prior professional preparation and experience.

2. There are specific assessment policies and procedures to ensure that applicants have adequate backgrounds and experience in middle level education.

3. Programs leading to the specialists in middle level education include the following:

    3.1 Major theories and research findings concerning early adolescent development: physical, social, emotional, intellectual, and moral.

    3.2 The history, philosophy, and future development of middle level education.

    3.3 Curriculum theories and research focusing on the middle level.

    3.4 Pedagogy appropriate for early adolescent learner.

    3.5 Advanced study in one or more board teaching fields.

    3.6 Study of educational leadership roles.

    3.7 A culminating project which demonstrates the candidate's leadership by applying middle level principles in the field.

DOCTORAL

1. The curriculum for the doctoral degree shows depth and breath in the study of the theoretical base and exemplary practice of middle level education. The plan of study for each student builds upon prior professional preparation and experience.

2. There are specific assessment policies and procedures to ensure that applicants have adequate backgrounds and experience in middle level education.

3. Programs leading to the doctorate in middle level education include the following components:

    3.1 An in-depth understanding and synthesis of:

        3.1.1 Major theories and research findings concerning early adolescent development: physical, social, emotional, intellectual, and moral.

3.1.2   The history, philosophy, and future development of middle level education.

3.1.3   Curriculum theories and research focusing on the middle level.

3.1.4   Pedagogy appropriate for early adolescent learners.

3.1.5   Adult development and learning.

3.2   Advanced study in one or more areas of specialization

3.3   Professional preparation for leadership roles in middle level education.

3.4   Research methodologies applied to middle level education

3.5   Dissertation or equivalent scholarly work which involves basic or applied research and study pertaining to middle level education.

APPENDIX B

Revised NMSA/NCATE-Approved Teacher Education Curriculum Guidelines

BASIC

1. Identifiable Program

An identifiable program is established for prospective middle level teachers.

> 1.1 A written conceptual framework makes explicit the underlying professional commitments, dispositions, and values upon which the program is based. A statement of philosophy and goals, associated rationale for course work and field experiences, and a description of program evaluation are included.

> 1.2 The program contains knowledge, pedagogy, and field experiences designed especially for teaching at the middle level.

2. Nature of Early Adolescence and Needs of Young Adolescents. The program prepares professionals who understand:

> 2.1 The physical, social, emotional, intellectual, and moral characteristics of the developmental period of early adolescence within social and cultural contexts.

> 2.2 The changes in family settings, social contexts, threats to health and safety, and risk behaviors in contemporary society that affect healthy development of young adolescents.

3. Young Adolescent Development in the School Context.

The program prepares professionals who apply their knowledge of the nature of early adolescence and needs of young adolescents to:

    3.1 Plan developmentally and culturally responsive instruction.

    3.2 Design appropriate school programs and function within them.

    3.3 Create supportive school environments.

4. Philosophy and School Organization. The program prepares professionals who understand the rationale for, the role of teachers in, and the function of:

    4.1 Interdisciplinary teams.

    4.2 Teacher-based guidance programs.

    4.3 Flexible grouping and scheduling arrangements.

    4.4 Activity programs.

    4.5 Working with colleagues within the framework of the entire school community.

    4.6 Working with families, resource persons, and community groups.

5. Curriculum, Pedagogy, and Assessment. The program prepares professionals who design and employ teaching and learning approaches appropriate for young adolescents which:

    5.1 Honor individual differences among learners by utilizing multiple approaches to thinking and learning.

    5.2 Incorporate leaders' ideas, interests, and questions into the exploration of curriculum and pursuit of knowledge.

    5.3 Emphasize the interdisciplinary nature of knowledge while drawing upon the resources inherent in separate subjects.

    5.4 Teach the basic concepts and skills of inquiry and communication as integral to all learning.

    5.5 Cultivate skills in recognizing and solving problems.

5.6 Utilize multiple grouping strategies that emphasize interdependence, cooperation, and individual responsibilities.

5.7 Employ accountability measures that balance evaluation of academic learning with assessment of individual growth and development.

5.8 Include multiple strategies for evaluation and assessment.

6. Collaboration The program prepares professionals who collaborate with:

6.1 Colleagues to improve schools and advance knowledge and practice in their fields.

6.2 Families, resource persons, and community groups to achieve common goals for young adolescents.

7. Teaching Fields and Pedagogy. The program includes:

7.1 Preparation in two teaching fields which are broad, multidisciplinary, and encompass the major areas within those fields.

7.2 At least one course designed specifically for teaching pedagogy appropriate for young adolescents.

8. Field Experiences. Field experiences in grades 5-8 will provide:

8.1 Early and continuing involvement in a variety of middle level settings.

8.2 Observation, participation, and teaching experiences ranging from individual to large group settings.

8.3 Full-time student teaching of at least 10 weeks, supervised by a qualified teacher and a university/college supervisor.

MASTERS

1. **Masters Program**

    1.1 A written conceptual framework makes explicit the underlying professional commitments, dispositions, and values upon which the program is based. A statement of philosophy and goals, an associated rationale for course work, and a description of program evaluation are included.

    1.2 The curriculum for the masters degree shows depth and breadth in the study of the theoretical base, research, and exemplary practice of middle level education.

    1.3 Each candidate's plan of study reflects prior professional preparation and experience.

Programs leading to the masters degree in middle level education include the following components:

2. **Early Adolescence in Contemporary Society**

    2.1 Theories and research concerning young adolescent development within cultural and social contexts.

    2.2 Theories and research relevant to changes in family settings, threats to health and safety, and risk behaviors that affect the healthy development of young adolescents.

3. **Philosophy and Organization**

    3.1 The history and philosophy of middle level education and theories about its future development.

    3.2 Theories, research, and exemplary practice concerning the organizational components of middle level schools.

3.3 Theories, research, and exemplary practice of program assessment and evaluation applied to middle level settings.

4. **Curriculum, Pedagogy, and Assessment**
   4.1 Theories, research, and exemplary practice focusing on middle level curriculum.
   4.2 Pedagogical theory, research, and exemplary practice appropriate for young adolescents.
   4.3 Theories, research, and exemplary practice regarding multiple approaches to the assessment and evaluation of learning.

5. **Teaching Fields and Applied Research**
   5.1 Advanced study in one or more teaching fields.
   5.2 A culminating examination, project, or thesis focusing on middle level education that links theory, research, and practice.

SPECIALIST

1. **Specialist Program**
   1.1 A written conceptual framework makes explicit the underlying professional commitments, dispositions, and values upon which the program is based. A statement of philosophy and goals, an associated rationale for course work, and a description of program evaluation are included.
   1.2 The curriculum for the specialist degree shows depth and breadth in the study of the theoretical base, research, and exemplary practice of middle level education.
   1.3 Specific assessment policies and procedures ensure that candidates have adequate professional preparation and experiences in middle level education.

1.4 Each candidate's plan of study reflects prior professional preparation and experience.

Programs leading to the specialist degree in middle level education include the following components:

2. **Early Adolescence in Contemporary Society**
   2.1 Theories and research concerning young adolescent development within social and cultural contexts.
   2.2 Theories and research relevant to changes in family settings, threats to health and safety, and risk behaviors that affect the healthy development of young adolescents.

3. **Philosophy and Organization**
   3.1 The history and philosophy of middle level education and theories about its future development.
   3.2 Theories, research, and exemplary practice concerning the organizational components of middle level schools.
   3.3 Theories, research, and exemplary practice of program assessment and evaluation applied to middle level settings.

4. **Curriculum, Pedagogy, and Assessment**
   4.1 Theories, research, and exemplary practice focusing on middle level curriculum.
   4.2 Pedagogical theories, research, and exemplary practice appropriate for young adolescents.
   4.3 Theories, research, and exemplary practice regarding multiple approaches to the assessment and evaluation of learning.

5. **Areas of Specialization and Educational Leadership**
   5.1 Advanced study in one or more areas of specialization.

5.2 Study of educational leadership roles.

5.3 Theory, research, and pedagogy regarding adult development and learning.

5.4 Theory and research on teacher development.

5.5 A culminating project which demonstrates the candidate's leadership by applying middle level principles in the field.

DOCTORAL

1. **Doctoral Program**

    1.1 A written conceptual framework makes explicit the underlying professional commitments, dispositions, and values upon which the program is based. A statement of philosophy and goals, an associated rationale for course work, and a description of program evaluation are included.

    1.2 The curriculum for the doctoral degree shows depth and breadth in the study of the theoretical base, research, and exemplary practice of middle level education.

    1.3 Specific assessment policies and procedures ensure that candidates have adequate professional preparation and experience in middle level education.

    1.4 Each candidate's plan of study reflects prior professional preparation and experience.

Programs leading to the doctoral degree in middle level education emphasize an in-depth understanding and synthesis of the following components:

2. **Early Adolescence in Contemporary Society**

    2.1 Theories and research concerning young adolescent development within social and cultural contexts.

2.2 Theories and research relevant to changes in family settings, threats to health and safety, and risk behavior that affect the healthy development of young adolescents.

3. **The Middle Level Teacher**
   3.1 Theory and research regarding adult development and learning.
   3.2 Pedagogy for adult learners.
   3.3 Theory and research on teacher development.
   3.4 Issues which affect middle level teachers.

4. **Philosophy and Organization**
   4.1 The history and philosophy of middle level education and theories about its future development.
   4.2 Theories, research, and exemplary practice concerning the organizational components of middle level schools.
   4.3 Theories, research, and exemplary practice of program assessment and evaluation applied to middle level settings.

5. **Curriculum, Pedagogy, and Assessment**
   5.1 Theories, research, and exemplary practice focusing on middle level curriculum.
   5.2 Pedagogical theory, research, and exemplary practice appropriate for young adolescents.
   5.3 Theories, research, and exemplary practice regarding multiple approaches to the assessment and evaluation of learning.

6. **Specialization, Leadership, and Research**
   6.1 Advanced study in one or more areas of specialization.

COMPARISON REVISED & ORIGINAL
NMSA/NCATE DOCTORAL GUIDELINES

1995 Revised Guidelines	1989 Original Guidelines	Type of Changes
1.1	—	New
1.2	1	Expanded
1.3	2	Expanded
1.4	1	Expanded
2.1	3.1.1	Clarified
2.2	—	New
3.1	3.1.5	Expanded
3.2	3.1.5	Expanded
3.3	—	New
3.4	—	New
4.1	3.1.2	Same
4.2	—	New
4.3	—	New
5.1	3.1.3	Clarified
5.2	3.1.4	Clarified
5.3	—	New
6.1	3.2	Same
6.2	3.3	Same
6.3	3.4	Same
6.4	3.5	Same